Strange Fruit

Rawle Agard

Strange Fruit

Race, Racial Profiling, and the Myth of Official Multiculturalism in the Canadian Imaginary

VDM Verlag Dr. Müller

Imprint

Bibliographic information by the German National Library: The German National Library lists this publication at the German National Bibliography; detailed bibliographic information is available on the Internet at http://dnb.d-nb.de.

Any brand names and product names mentioned in this book are subject to trademark, brand or patent protection and are trademarks or registered trademarks of their respective holders. The use of brand names, product names, common names, trade names, product descriptions etc. even without a particular marking in this works is in no way to be construed to mean that such names may be regarded as unrestricted in respect of trademark and brand protection legislation and could thus be used by anyone.

Cover image: www.purestockx.com

Publisher:
VDM Verlag Dr. Müller Aktiengesellschaft & Co. KG, Dudweiler Landstr. 125 a, 66123 Saarbrücken, Germany,
Phone +49 681 9100-698, Fax +49 681 9100-988,
Email: info@vdm-verlag.de

Copyright © 2008 VDM Verlag Dr. Müller Aktiengesellschaft & Co. KG and licensors
All rights reserved. Saarbrücken 2008

Produced in USA and UK by:
Lightning Source Inc., La Vergne, Tennessee, USA
Lightning Source UK Ltd., Milton Keynes, UK
BookSurge LLC, 5341 Dorchester Road, Suite 16, North Charleston, SC 29418, USA

ISBN: 978-3-639-04402-7

Abstract

This thesis investigates the concept of 'race' and its place within the discourse of 'official multiculturalism' in the Canadian context. More specifically, I explore the ways that 'race' has been coded in the popular media in my examination of selected articles from the *Toronto Star's* coverage of: Philippe Rushton, human genome research, and racial profiling practiced by the Toronto Police Service. Through a textual analysis that combines the insights of Barthes'(1972) notion of myth as well as tools derived from critical discourse analysis, this research reveals that a conservative racialized discourse lies beneath *The Star's* seemingly critical stance on issues of racism. Indeed, although *The Star* appears, ostensibly, to be critical of racism it, nonetheless, maintains and perpetuates dominant perceptions of 'race' as both an objective genetic entity and a permanent category that exists in culture.

Despite my findings and the fact that most progressive social scientists refrain from employing the construct of 'race' as a determinant of specific social phenomena, discussions of 'race' – as a fixed analytical and descriptive category – continue to dominate popular and media discourses. Such rigid characterizations are also prevalent in the official narratives of Canadian multiculturalism that attempt to define and categorize citizens into clearly delineable groupings under the rubric of 'difference'. This notion of 'difference', couched in the broader 'liberal' discourse of tolerance and diversity, however, continues to reinscribe 'race' as a fixed cultural category. Moreover, such formulations tend to contain the vestiges of colonialist legacies.

In order to dismantle the 'strange fruits' that 'racisms' bear within today's multicultural society, one must first understand, and then demystify the common myth about 'race' as a social and historical construct imbedded in the colonialist ideologies of imperial domination as they are imbricated in the policies and practices of 'official multiculturalism' in Canada. This undertaking must be premised on the notion that the modern concept of 'race' comes out of the existence of racism and not vice versa. Indeed, the popular concept of 'race' must be reconsidered if any meaningful anti-racist discourse is to be articulated and put into the broader aims of social justice.

Acknowledgements

I would like to thank Dr. Irvin Goldman for his guidance and wisdom throughout my scholarly journey. His enthusiasm for the material covered in this thesis is a testament to his hard work and dedication to the study of communication that is reflected in my own enthusiasm for continued scholarship in this vast field.

My other co-advisor, Dr. James Winter, was very keen on my academic development over the past two years. He has been a great source of enlightenment on various issues of media literacy, contributing to my growth as a critical scholar through both his graduate seminar and his sharp counsel. I am especially indebted to his insightful suggestions throughout the duration of this project.

Although she was invited to take a position on this committee late in this project's development, Dr. Valerie Scatamburlo D'Annibale has been a guiding inspiration from the outset of this task. I am eternally grateful for her wisdom and passion for teaching and learning that has enabled her to provide helpful suggestions and feedback for my research even when she did not have to. Her vast knowledge and insights on a seemingly endless array of subjects cannot be overlooked in the work that follows.

At times when I would find myself tangled in the theoretical web of my own research, Professor Leigh West was an excellent source of questions and criticisms that helped ground my work, influencing me to be more conscious of potential readers outside of this department in my writing.

Although he was not on my committee and I had no classes with him, Dr. Garth Rennie provided me with valuable sources that were critical in formulating some key issues found in this thesis. His positive energy throughout this process was unmatched.

Indeed, I am indebted to Sandy Van Zetten, Anne Gallant, and Sharon Wazny for helping me with some of my departmental and administrative queries. These individuals have made the detailed tasks involved with graduate life all the more easier.

I would like to make a special mention to Dr. Marlene Cuthbert and Dr. Kai Hildebrandt. Their support and wisdom has been a great influence to me while I was an undergraduate student. As a result, their continued encouragement has sparked my desire to continue further into an academic career.

Moreover, a section on acknowledgements could not be complete without mentioning the company of colleagues that have been with me throughout this graduate school adventure. Of this brilliant group of young scholars I would like to extend a special mention to: Leif Schumacher, Jeremy Marentette, Maya Ruggles, Lisa Bastien, and Irena Knezevic. Our discussions on a varied array of topics have been priceless in this journey that we have embarked on together. Of this group Leif Schumacher deserves particular thanks as he has been especially helpful in the editing stages of this work. I am grateful for his selfless efforts and friendship along the way.

Last but not least, I would like to thank my friends and family. Gail Agard, Rawle Agard Sr., Beryl Wilson, Edna Agard, Dwayne Matthews, Brian Ward, Jeffrey Hyles, Warren Hamer, Gary Whittingham, Sean Agard, Michelle Agard, Dr. George Bancroft, Damien Boucaud, Jennifer Swart. Knowing that I have such a strong foundation of family and friends fuels my motivation and impels my desire towards continued success. Thank you all for everything you have given me that continues to make me who I am.

TABLE OF CONTENTS

Abstract   iv

Acknowledgements   vi

CHAPTER

I. IN THE BEGINING

STRANGE FRUIT –
A Naturalized, Normalizing Discourse   1

BIOPOWER –
Life & Death; The Struggle to Survive   3

TIME AFTER TIME –
That was then. This is now   6

THE STRUCTURE OF OPPRESSION –
Behind a 'Few Bad Apples'   9

STATE RACISM –
A Collective Cultural Concept   12

A NEW RIGHT RATIONALIZATION –
'Race' and Cultural DNA   13

DERACINATING 'RACE' –
Towards a Libratory Anti-Racism Discourse   15

II. O' CANADA…OUR HOME ON NATIVE LAND?

A PARADOX OF BELONGING –
The Construction of a Common Canadian   18

TWO SIDES OF THE SAME COIN –
Metaphors 'Melting Pot' and 'Mosaic'   20

III. LOCATING CULTURE IN MULTICULTURE

PERPETUALLY RECEDING HORIZONS –
Constructing Cultural Imaginings   24

	MULTICULTURALISM AND THE CONFINEMENT OF CULTURE	26
	DEHUMANIZING OBJECTS OF DIFFERENCE AND A CULT OF FETISH	28
	MULTICULTURAL MOSAIC – Centre & Periphery Reborn in the 'Ex-factor'	31
IV.	**HISTORICAL CONTINGENCIES TO RACIALIZED REALITIES**	
	LANGUAGE OF RELATIONAL DIFFERENCES – 'Race' of Ancients to Irish	37
	EMPIRE AND THE BIRTH OF 'RACE' AS A BIOLOGICAL TAXONOMY	41
	'PECULIAR INSTITUTIONS' AND THE PRODUCTION OF RACISMS	42
	PUTTING THE 'CRITICAL' BACK IN CRITICAL RACE THEORIES	44
	'RACE' vs. 'RACIALIZED COMMUNITIES' – Demystification & Emphasis	46
	THE NATURE OF THINGS – Grouping Populations According to 'Race'?	47
	SLIDING SIGNIFICATIONS AND THE LANGUAGE OF 'RACE'	49
V.	**THE SCIENCE OF OPPRESSION**	
	COMPETING SCIENTIFIC PARADIGMS – A Contested Terrain of Inquiry	54
	J. PHILIPPE RUSHTON AND THE EVOLUTIONARY PARADOX	55
	GENETICS OF 'RACE' – Science Fact or Fiction?	70
VI.	**LIVING THROUGH LANGUAGE**	
	REALITY & 'RACE' – Making Sense of Our Existence through Language	77

	LANGUAGE & DISCOURSE – A Brief Description	78
	CONCEPTUALIZING IDEOLOGY – From Ideas to Practice to Resistance	79
	THE SEMIOTICS OF MYTH – Meaning & the Process of Signification	83
	DISCOURSE - A MYTHIC META-LANGUAGE	91
VII.	**CRITICAL DISCOURSE ANALYSIS**	
	THEORY AND METHODOLOGY REVISITED – From Semiotics to CDA	93
	THE ROLE OF DISCOURSE & POWER IN CRITICAL ANALYSIS	94
	MYTH, IDEOLOGY, KNOWLEDGE – Multidisciplinary Discursive Approach	100
	THE FLEXIBLE QUALITY OF CDA – A Malleable Methodological Approach	104
	LEVELS OF ANALYSIS – A Multi-layered Technique	105
	TOOLS OF THE TRADE FOR "TEXT AND TALK"	107
VIII.	**A MEDIATED STREAM OF CONSCIOUSNESS**	
	REALITY AND THE MEDIA'S PRODUCTION OF PERCEPTION	110
	MASS MEDIA AND MASS AUDIENCES – Homogeneity to Heterogeneity	112
	UNIVERSE AND OR MULTIVERSE – A Many Sided Reality	113
	ACTIVE AUDIENCE AND THE POWER OF MEDIA – Negotiated Dominance	114

IX.	**ANALYSIS OF INCORPORATED RESISTENCE**	
	CONSERVATIVE IDEOLOGIES AND THE LIBERAL MEDIA	117
	CDA – An Applied Methodology	117
	EXISTENCE OF RACIAL PROFILING – Does it Occur in TPS Practices?	121
	COLOUR-CODED – Visualizing 'Race' and the Perpetuation of Myth	126
X.	**MOVING BEYOND 'RACE'**	
	CONCLUSION – Putting to rest the 'Strange Fruits' of our Past in the Present	139

References 146

Appendix 160

Vita Auctoris 162

I. IN THE BEGINNING

STRANGE FRUIT – A Naturalized, Normalizing Discourse

> *Southern trees bear strange fruit,*
> *Blood on the leaves and blood at the root,*
> *Black bodies swinging in the southern breeze,*
> *Strange fruit hanging from the poplar trees.*
>
> *Pastoral scene of the gallant south,*
> *The bulging eyes and the twisted mouth,*
> *Scent of magnolias, sweet and fresh,*
> *Then the sudden smell of burning flesh.*
>
> *Here is fruit for the crows to pluck,*
> *For the rain to gather, for the wind to suck,*
> *For the sun to rot, for the trees to drop,*
> *Here is a strange and bitter crop.*
>
> (Abel Meeropol AKA Lewis Allen 1939)

Inspired by the overt racism entrenched in the culture of the 'deep south' (USA), a young patron of Harlem's trendy Café Society wrote a haunting poem on lynching as a represented manifestation of American social injustice in hopes that it would be performed by Billie Holliday. Little did he know the impact that his poem would have on the world of jazz, blues, popular culture, and – for the purposes of this thesis – a critical theory about 'race' and its relation to multicultural society. Although composed to articulate the racism of a seemingly bygone era, its spectre still haunts new articulations of the 'racisms'[1] that plaque society today.

---

11 Borrowing from Antonia Darder and Rudolfo Torres (2004), I ocasionally refer to racism in the plural. 'Racisms', as opposed to racism, is conceptualized "within the context of demographic shifts, changing capitalist class relations, and global socioeconomic dislocations" (Darder & Torres, 2004, p. 3). This pluralized conceptualization of 'racisms' is better suited than its singularized counterpart for theorizing about the premise that 'race' is not a fixed entity. In light of this fact 'race' will be frequently typed in quotation to draw attention to its arbitrary quality. Attempts to fix 'race' in science, religion, culture etc., has resulted in a popularized concept of racism that has been antiquated amidst the changing order of various social phenomena both locally and globally. In contrast, 'Racisms' serve to encompass change while preventing static understandings of racialized oppressions from being relegated to the dustbins of a colonial and separatist past. As a result, 'racisms' can be seen to take many forms in society today that not only accounts for individual acts but also systemic forms of oppression.

As today's society becomes increasingly diverse, it may seem absurd at first glance, to level the accusation that these 'strange fruits' still continue to grow. Certainly, lynching does not occur in a 'liberal' and arguably progressive place like Canada. What, then, of these 'strange fruit'? And how are they relevant to the study of 'race' and 'racisms' in today's multicultural society? In order to address this accusation, one must first take a critical look at the discourse that lines the narrative of this poem's verses.

The pastoral imagery of this poem displays a paradox of values in a society where identity is constructed between the narratives of a performative dialectic – a dialect performed between the voice of 'self' and 'other'; 'us' and 'them'; 'Western[2] (European) Occidental white' and 'Non-Western (non- European) Oriental people of colour'. Identities of 'self' and 'other' are constructed amidst this play of difference. A relationship of power is formed in the hierarchical categorization of this difference that interpolates the former in a position of dominance over the subjugated latter. Following in the deep rooted ideologies of colonial 'racisms' that plague contemporary social relations, a crisis of identity occurs in the location of 'self' through the displacement of 'other' (Bannerji, 2000; Darder & Torres, 2004; Eze, 2001; Hardt & Negri, 2000; Razack, 2004; Said, 1978, 1993; San Juan Jr., 2002; Walcott, 2003).

In this instance, 'self' comes into existence through the violence perpetuated on the populations of 'other' as a sure way of demarcating difference. It is assumed then, that in order for 'self' to exist, populations of 'other' that exist within the national landscape must be categorized and strictly policed (Clarke, 1993; Razack, 2004; Said, 1978, 1993; Walcott, 2003). By policing 'other', especially through violence, order in

---

[2] Throughout this thesis, I will often refer to 'Western' – not narrowly defined as a cultural singularity – but as a hybrid and heterogeneous Empire derived from dominant/ ruling classes of imperialist European values.

society is established as natural. Indeed this is made explicit by virtue of the 'strange fruit' (i.e. the dangling black bodies amidst the sweet fragrance of magnolias). The imagery depicts a seemingly natural occurring phenomena (the growth of dangling black bodies on the southern trees) hitherto unquestioned, and taken for granted as an ornamental part of the common landscape. Difference becomes fixed as lifeless; open to the gaze and consumption of the dominant, conquering, colonizing status quo.

In her book, *Regarding the Pain of Others,* Susan Sontag (2003) illustrates the seemingly natural qualities of this discourse by describing how the 'pain of others' is viewed or 'examined'[3] through the privileged lens of the 'self'. Referring to the photographs taken of 'black victims of lynching', and the subsequent spectacle that ensued after its publication in book format, Sontag (2003) critically explores the act of indulging in these representations to help the viewer/examiner understand the acts depicted "not as the acts of 'barbarians' but as the reflection of a belief system, racism, that by defining one people as less human than another legitimates torture and murder" (p. 92). Racism, in this sense, is not a simple act of deviance or isolated practices. Indeed, racism exists as a functional part of everyday society. This is the result of what Foucault (2003) refers to when he claims that 'biopower' becomes celebrated within the 'mechanisms of the State'.

BIOPOWER – Life & Death; The Struggle to Survive

According to Michel Foucault (2003), modern racism – practiced through the State – takes the form of what he calls 'biopower'. For Foucault, 'biopower' – as a basic

---

[3] For Susan Sontag (2003), the significance of the term 'examine' is given a sense of agency on the part of the viewer to 'clinically' or perhaps critically indulge in as opposed to simply 'look at' the images depicted. This is an attempt to resolve any feelings of guilt or voyeuristic pleasure from inadvertently part-taking, second-hand, in the atrocities and suffering of 'others' as they were depicted (p. 92).

mechanism of power – essentially forms a break in the biological continuum, creating the existence of separate 'races' from one; the human 'race'. In the process of distinguishing differences between separate 'races', a hierarchy among them is formed determined by imagined qualities of superiority and inferiority. By fragmenting an otherwise unified biological domain into separate 'races', power becomes distributed unevenly throughout. Because of this, racism is seen to have two functions.

First, racism functions to fragment society in the interests of maintaining an unequal distribution of power among populations. Second, as a result of 'biopower', racism functions to purify those considered to be members of superior 'races' – as an act of survival – by annihilating those whom it considers to be members of inferior 'races'. Like the images in *Strange Fruit*, difference must be separated, managed, and controlled through the practice of 'biopower' in the interests of maintaining the existence of an imagined 'superior race'. In the process, subjugated 'races' become isolated from the state mechanisms that define and exhibit power over them, causing a type of civic death deemed necessary to preserve the civic life of the 'superior races'. Bridging the gap between the violent effects of yesterday's racism – as seen through lynching – to the more contemporary forms of racism – like 'official multiculturalism' and racial profiling – Foucault (2003) is worth quoting at length here:

> In a normalizing society, race or racism is the precondition that makes killing acceptable. When you have a normalizing society, you have a power which is, at least superficially, in the first instance, or in the first line a biopower, and racism is the indispensable precondition that allows someone to be killed, that allows others to be killed. Once the State functions in the biopower mode, racism alone can justify the murderous function of the State…If the power of normalization wished to exercise the old sovereign right to kill, it must become racist. And if, conversely, a power of sovereignty, or in other words, a power that has the right of life and death, wishes to work with the instruments, mechanisms, and technology of normalization, it too must become racist. (p. 256)

The above passage can be interpreted to explicitly explain the way racism works through 'biopower' – the power over life and death – in a naturalized environment like the one described in *Strange Fruit*. It can also be interpreted to implicitly explain the ways in which 'racisms' continues to work through 'biopower' today – without the overt violence of lynching – through the State mechanisms of 'official multiculturalism' and racial profiling. This can be seen when Foucault (2003) goes on to explain that the meanings behind killing and murder, as justifiable actions within a 'normalizing society', can be taken both literally and figuratively. Life and death are qualities of 'biopower' that are no longer considered absolute; they become notions relative to the imagined boundaries created in discourse.

> When I say "killing," I obviously do not mean simply murder as such, but also every form of indirect murder: the fact of exposing someone to death, increasing the risk of death for some people, or, quite simply, political death, expulsion, rejection and so on…And we can also understand why racism should have developed in modern societies that function in the biopower mode…Racism first develops with colonization, or in other words with colonizing genocide. (Foucault, 2003, pp. 256-257)

The above passages clarify the functions of racism – rooted in colonialism – that essentially works through 'biopower' in a normalizing capacity, exercising control over life and death among populations. This normalizing capacity creates the existence of a social order that is made to look natural. Through naturalization of this social order, the gaps of inequality and injustice become obscured. As a result, when further applied to the poem *Strange Fruit*, the 'strange fruit' – as physical manifestations of the function of racism ('race') – are tolerated as objectified parts of the social landscape. This is a reminder, albeit extreme, as to how this society is at the same time tolerant and intolerant of difference in the spectacle of identity construction. If we deconstruct this narrative further, it becomes evident that the Southern trees (racism) bear 'strange fruit' (historical and material effects of its harmful discourse through 'race') that marks the imagined identity of the colonized world.

Strange Fruit happens to be the title of this thesis for what I believe to be very current and salient reasons. I use this title because I plan to illustrate that the 'tree' of racism continues to bear 'strange fruit' of injustice and oppression despite the fact that overt and physical manifestations like lynching in a presumably 'liberal' society such as Canada, are now rare. Even though the violence of overt forms of racisms are rare today, more sophisticated and subtle acts of violence have evolved through 'biopower' to effectively control life and death, symbolically, in the realms of social and political struggle. Indeed, as an historical phenomenon, vestiges of the past continue to linger and inform the present. In order to understand this point better, a critical perspective on the conception of time must be elucidated.

TIME AFTER TIME – That was then. This is now.

Time is not necessarily linear and intermittent nor is it essentially classified by increments defined in space and cultural achievement that carry clear demarcations in history. How we interpret our existence by virtue of its temporality is largely a cultural undertaking. Referring to T.S. Eliot's central premise on the relationship between past, present, and future, Edward Said (1993) states that "how we formulate or represent the past shapes our understanding and view of the present" (p. 4). Under this conception of time, past and present are overlapping qualities. There is a large degree of the past in the present. Because of this, the legacy of colonialism persists today through the totalizing ideological tenets of imperialism.

Edward Said (1993), in his book *Culture and Imperialism*, picks up where *Orientalism* leaves off in its central question as to whether or not modern imperialism has ended with colonialism. In this book Said (1993) articulates clear definitions of colonialism and imperialism as historical agents of domination that I find applicable in discussing the management of difference today. According to Said (1993), "imperialism means the practice, the theory, and the attitudes of a dominating metropolitan centre ruling a distant territory; colonialism, which is almost always a consequence of imperialism, is the implanting of settlements on a distant territory" (p. 9). However narrowly defined on one level, these notions imply a spatial metaphor grounded in the acquisition of foreign territory – foreign in respect to the positioning the imperial centre in relation to the conquered periphery. By virtue of this understanding, colonialism as a consequence of imperialism – where settlements are erected in geographical space – is not as common today. The colonialism of the past, however, has now been transformed into a neo-colonialism of the present – where settlements are erected in social, cultural, political and economic spaces – continuing an imperial legacy of domination and oppression.

Applying contemporary notions of imperialism and colonialism to more current issues regarding the management of diversity, it becomes evident that imperialism and colonialism can imply more than mere accumulation and control of geographical space. Indeed, these terms can be interpreted to represent the accumulation and control of cultures. For example, the centre/ periphery metaphor still holds true under the 'impressive ideological formations'[4], which have become institutionalized in state policy

---

4 By using the phrase "impressive ideological formations", Edward Said (1993, p. 9) refers to the structures and or mechanisms that support and drive imperialism and colonialism beyond the acts of

and public discourse, through the fixing and ordering of differences in the public sphere. Imperialism still persists in relation to its political, economic, and social capacities to subjugate marginalized groups of diverse populations residing within the conquered periphery. In sum, as the past and present are intimately related and overlapping, the 'impressive ideological formations' of a colonial legacy are passed on from a colonial history of imperialistic exploits that continue to manifest in current social circumstances.

Thomas Holt (2000) illustrates this phenomenon clearly by stating that "the tropes of racism are fairly constant whereas the repertoire of racist practices is all too mutable" (p. 27). Within the context of *Strange Fruit,* a history of marked physical subjugations – like lynching – are transformed into more subtle acts of social and political disenfranchisement as seen in today's more polite, institutionalised 'racisms' that systematically mark and segregate difference. This distinction is what Stuart Hall (1995) refers to as 'overt' and 'inferential' racism. The latter form of racism, constitutive of a naturalized sate of mind, has become so ingrained in the every day functioning of society that it often works to name and defeat the former type of racism as deviant (Essed, 2002). In so doing, it essentially masks and obscures its own racist actions. This latter racism is what Paul Street (2002) refers to as 'New Age Racism'. Although individual acts of overt racism still exist, they have declined considerably as a result of the growing strength of 'New Age Racism' (Street, 2002). In my opinion, therefore, the more subtle and arguably more impressionable nuances of institutional 'racisms' have become increasingly deserving of our attention within a purportedly tolerant and increasingly diverse society.

---

acquiring objects (land and people). For Said (1993) these structures and mechanisms "include notions that certain territories and people *require* and beseech domination, as well as forms of knowledge affiliated with domination" (p. 9).

In a 1992 essay titled "Public Enemies", Austin Clarke poignantly outlines this concern by stating the importance of analyzing the structure of racism over individual acts. "I am not speaking about private, individual intercourse. I am speaking, rather, about the entire system, that institutional structure of unapproachable, unseen power" (Clarke, 1992, p.11). While addressing the issues of police violence against racialized communities, Clarke goes beyond engaging in the discourse of racism as merely isolated and individual occurrences by placing the entire system of racism under scrutiny. For Clarke, although these individual acts deserve our serious attention, they should not detract from or obscure our focus on the 'institutional structure' that lay beneath such acts. This is precisely where he believes the true power of racism resides.

THE STRUCTURE OF OPPRESSION – Behind 'A Few Bad Apples'

Analyzing the structural dynamics of racism, this thesis focuses on the institutional forms that I believe to be more insidious than the overt acts of 'a few bad apples'[5]. I consider institutional racism to be more insidious precisely due to the fact that it has become a naturalized and functioning part of our current multicultural society. Take for instance, the brutal torture and beating of a Somali youth by two members of the Canadian Peacekeeping forces during the UN intervention of 1992. Sherene Razack

---

5 The term 'a few bad apples' refers to the overt, pathological, and more or less criminal actions of individuals – now considered deviant in today's 'liberal' society – that champion the beliefs of white supremacy. It is worthy to note here that Windsor's Chief of Police, Glen Stannard, at an October 25th 2003 panel discussion on racial profiling put on by the Local 200 CAW, acknowledged that racism exists within the police service, not in the capacity that the Windsor Police service is a racist organization or that systemic racism exits within the institution per se but to the effect that there have been incidents caused by 'a few bad apples' that tarnish the services reputation. Chief Stannard made it clear that these 'bad apples' have made community-oriented policing more difficult and wished to work with the community to put an end to it. By limiting the definition of racism to the actions of 'a few bad apples', the Windsor Police Chief surreptitiously avoided the implications that his service may be involved in the practice of racial profiling, while discounting the existence of broader systemic racisms as a pervasive part of our everyday lives. This makes the task of ending institutional racisms all the more elusive when the structure of every day racism, that plague society, are stifled from the onset, preventing any meaningful discussion towards a solution.

(2004) illustrates the fact that although these racist actions appear on the surface to be exceptional with regards to Canada's peacekeeping initiatives; they speak directly to the hidden racisms that underlie Canada's colonial legacy as bearing the 'white man's burden' of executing the civilizing mission in the 'darkest corners' of the earth.

The fact that the two soldiers implicated in the beating death of Shidane Arone – the murdered Somali youth – were of Aboriginal origin – also members of an oppressed class – increases the importance of examining the incident as not wholly exceptional but sutured deep within the everyday consciousness of the troops deployed to bring peace to an otherwise 'savage and barbaric land'. According to Razack (2004 a), "to look for exceptional and overtly racist acts was to miss the absolute ordinariness and pervasiveness of the racist attitudes and practices both in the military generally and among the troops deployed in Somalia" (p. 126). Although the Canadian military did have self-declared white supremacists among their ranks working in Somalia, few of these individuals were directly implicated in the events that transpired. This is crucial to understanding a broader definition of racism – as a structural belief system that signifies the power relationship of dominance and oppression based on phenotype or cultural superiority – and the subsequent dehumanization of the 'other' through the ideologies of colonialism and imperialism[6]. To extend this definition of racism, as a system of beliefs, a bit further, without alienating or excluding the practices that follow from such beliefs, racism can become broadly characterized as a way of life.

Racism, as a way of life, is not exclusively owned by devout pathological practitioners of racial discrimination, nor should it be limited to a narrow definition that

---

6 Sherene Razack (2004) advocates the use of a broad definition of racism to imply colonialism and imperialism. Borrowing from Said (1993), racism in this sense is "not simply the acquisition of lands but also the 'impressive ideological formations' that continue on into the present". (Razack, 2004, p. 143)

targets them exclusively. To solely focus on a narrow definition of the term would effectively sever the deeper historical hatreds and "the material and ideological systems" that thrive on them (Razack, 2004, p.135). Racism has a structure that is woven neatly amidst the dominant ways of viewing the world. Because of this, 'racisms' are more subtle and pervasive than commonly assumed. As a result they have become invisible, existing 'unseen' as a part of our everyday discourse (Clarke, 1992). Indeed, its effects on society, therefore, are not necessarily immediately evident.

    Racism, as a common part of everyday life, can be seen as working like microwave signals – invisible forces that can lead to critical illnesses having adverse effects on the human body when subject to prolonged periods of exposure. If we view society like a human body and racism like microwave signals, racism can be imagined to collect and fester within the social entity inevitably leading to social anomie, and ultimately social death. If left unchecked for long periods of time, racism can work like a cancer causing agent, slowly eating away at the very fabric of humanity that essentially binds a healthy and socially just civilization. Examples of how 'racisms' are currently working this way are illustrated in the police narratives of racial profiling that are fertilized by the 'liberal' discourses of tolerance and diversity which also form the foundation of Canada's notion of 'official multiculturalism'. Although the practice of racial profiling and multiculturalism are not as overt as scenes of lynching, 'racisms' continue to grow, masked beneath the seductive scent of 'official multiculturalism' that continues to be mystified in the Canadian identity – 'sweet and fresh'. They still produce 'strange fruit' as they are rooted in the soils of a racist colonial ideology.

STATE RACISM – A Collective Cultural Concept

> The discourse of race struggle ... will become the discourse of power itself. It will become the discourse of a centred, centralized and centralizing power. It will become the discourse of a battle that has to be waged not between races, but by a race that is portrayed as the one true race, the race that holds the power and is entitled to define the norm, and against those who deviate from that norm, against those who pose a threat to the biological heritage. At this point, we have all those biological-racist discourses of degeneracy, but also all those institutions within the social body which make the discourse of race struggle function as a principle of exclusion and segregation and, ultimately, as a way of normalizing society ... At this point ... we see the appearance of State racism: a racism that society will direct against itself, against its own elements and its own products. (Foucault, 2003, pp. 61-62)

'Racisms' – institutional and individual – are a common phenomenon within our contemporary multicultural society. 'Racisms' in Canada are common due to the fact that difference has been legitimated as a 'natural factor' in the production of the national imaginary[7]. This national imaginary appears to be altogether tolerant and inclusive of difference, through various political and economic apparatuses (official multiculturalism, affirmative action policies, and 'liberal' notions of capitalism etc.), while simultaneously retaining the colonial discourse of intolerance and exclusiveness (Hardt & Negri, 2000) through the process of 'otherizing' or 'orientalizing' difference (Said, 1978, 1993). Bearing the 'strange fruit' of injustice, this paradox indicates somewhat of a national identity crisis – rooted in an older colonial ideology of racism – that continues today through a 'liberal' discourse of tolerance and difference. This crisis of identity has created essentialized, fixed categories of people, further perpetuating a hierarchy of

---

[7] I use the adjective 'imaginary' to describe Canada as a national construct composed in the imagination of its citizens. I have borrowed this term to reflect a 'national imagination', or as Himmani Bannerji (2000) states (in the tradition of Benedict Anderson, 1991) a 'national imaginary'. Further reference to the use of this term can be found throughout her book *The Dark Side of the Nation*. Canada's 'national imaginary' can be found on page 65 in reference to a totality of collective imaginations. Richard Day (1998) outlines the mosaic metaphor, illustrating claims that Canadian identity is structured on a notion that Canadian history is multicultural. To quote Day (1998), "although this claim is obviously absurd, that hasn't prevented it from being a nodal signifier in the official Canadian imaginary" (p. 42)

difference structured in modern notions of 'race' and culture[8] (Bannerji, 2000; Bissoondath, 2002; Walcott, 2003).

'Race' as a biological and discursive analytical concept has also been recently subsumed by narrowly defined notions of culture (Darder & Torres, 2004; Hardt & Negri, 2000; Razack, 2004; San Juan Jr., 2002), that can be heard from both right-wing conservative voices (D'Souza, 1995) as well as those who speak from a more liberal pluralist ideology (Taylor, 1994). In both cases 'race' and/or culture serve as homogeneous fixtures that define, position, and manage populations in relational difference to one another. In some cases, 'race' and culture are often used interchangeably. This can be seen in the ways that cultural/ racial difference comes to overshadow cultural/ racial similarities in conservative discourse.

A NEW RIGHT RATIONALIZATION – 'Race' and Cultural DNA

According to Dinesh D'Souza (1995) people in general have more shared traits than differences overall. Despite this admission, however, he also believes it to be foolish to perceive these differences as insignificant. D'Souza (1995) claims that such

---

8 Although I occasionally cite criticisms of multiculturalism by including Neil Bissoondath, Himani Bannerji, Rinaldo Walcott and E. San Juan Jr. in the same reference, it is important to make note of the fact that their criticisms of multiculturalism come from opposing perspectives. Bissoondath's criticism of multiculturalism comes from a more conservative perspective that can often be coupled with writers such as Dinesh D'Souza. As a result, Bissoondath often appears to be hostile of immigrants who resist assimilation. For Bissoondath, the problem of multiculturalism is a problem of immigrants who refuse to assimilate within a presumably superior Eurocentric way of life. Contrary to Bissoondath, however, Bannerji and San Juan Jr. criticize multiculturalism with a more critical focus on the existence of a racialized political economy. From this perspective, the problem of multiculturalism is not due to a lack of assimilation from immigrants but the systematic exclusion and marginalization of divergent (immigrant) voices from the shaping of the political economy towards the benefit of all walks of life within a given citizenry. According to Bannerji and San Juan Jr., assimilation only serves to manage and police difference under the 'liberal' rubric of tolerance and diversity. Moreover, this perspective views multiculturalism as a form of apartheid, segregating citizens rather than uniting them. Despite these contrasting perspectives, there are some points of convergence that articulate ideas complimentary to their respective differences. One such notion of convergence can be seen in the ways that culture is viewed as a living thing that cannot be static or absolute. As a result, differences between cultures cannot be fixed. My intention behind citing these authors together within the same reference was to highlight this particular example of convergence without implying that they come from the same perspective.

differences, therefore, should not be overlooked. "Just as variation among individuals explains why some individuals perform better than others, so variation between groups could explain why some groups do better than others" (D'Souza, 1995, p. 450). Indeed, this statement addresses individual differences and group differences alike. The problem exists, however, in the uncertain attributes that distinguish the individual from the group.

Although D'Souza (1995) explores various theories on 'race' as naturally defined by biological attributes – many of which contradict each other – he does not clearly define his position on how groups should be distinguished from each other. Instead, he quietly escapes critically engaging the contradictory debate over biological determinism by simply stating that groups do in fact exist naturally without explaining how or why. Seeing that he cannot fix group differences to any one theory of biological distinction, D'Souza (1995) insists on the salience of cultural distinction by virtue of socialization and education as an – albeit tenuous – appendage to theories of natural selection. Culture, in this sense, becomes the 'new biology' as a matter of expression.

Culture as the 'new biology' does not imply biology in the clinical or scientific sense of the word but can be seen in the ways that groups of people are slotted into fixed homogeneous imaginaries of a new heredity, passed on from one generation to the next; a "cultural DNA" of sorts (D'Souza, 1995, p. 472). This 'cultural DNA' – evidence of fixed group differences championed by the new polite racists (Van Dijk, 1998, 2000, 2001) – serves to explain the 'pathologies' and sociable deficiencies of various cultural/ racial groupings in society (Podur, 2002). Furthering this perspective, Michael Hardt and Antonio Negri (2000) state that "as a theory of social difference, the cultural position is no less 'essentialist' than the biological one, or at least it establishes an equally strong theoretical ground for social separation and segregation" (p. 192). Accordingly, this 'cultural DNA', used by D'Souza (1995) and his neo-conservative epigones, has served to simultaneously justify and deny racism based on the notion of "rational discrimination" (p. 282).

'Rational discrimination' exists as a contradiction in terms whereby it has been used to justify policies that boldly legitimate institutional racisms like racial profiling, without actually admitting that there is such a thing as institutional racism. This is illustrated in D'Souza's (1995) belief that institutional racism implicates everybody, in some capacity, as being racist. D'Souza's (1995) faulty reasoning follows that "if everyone is a racist, then no one is a racist" (p. 335). This statement cleverly uses circular logic to mask oppression and promote "white complicity" (Razack, 2004a, p. 141) while obfuscating the historical and material conditions that enable racisms to exist.

DERACINATING 'RACE' – Towards a Libratory Anti-Racism Discourse

I believe that in order to dismantle racism one must explore the power relationships created by overt and individual racisms and their connection to the more subtle nuances of institutional 'racisms'. It is my contention that the modern concept of 'race' and its tenuous, albeit contemporary, connection to an erroneous perception of culture – must first be dissected and ameliorated from the chains of its objectified position in society at large, before being eradicated altogether, if any meaningful anti-racist discourse is to be articulated and put into practice in the interest of broader social justice aims. This undertaking must be premised on two levels.

First and foremost, the notion that the modern concept of 'race' comes out of the existence of racism, and not vice versa (Darder & Torres, 2004) must be clearly understood and accepted. And the reality of racism, in fact, has absolutely nothing to do with the existence of distinct 'races'. Second, a broader more transitional understanding of culture must be liberated from this outdated notion of 'race'. In order to dismantle the 'strange fruit' that racisms bear within today's multicultural society, one must first understand and demystify the modern myth about 'race' as a social and historical construct, imbedded in the colonialist ideologies of imperial domination, as they are imbricated in the policies and practices of 'official multiculturalism' in Canada.

This thesis investigates, in a preliminary way, the concept of 'race' and its place within the discourse of 'official multiculturalism' in the Canadian context. More specifically, the ways that 'race' has been 'coded' and 'represented' in the popular media through an examination of selected articles from the *Toronto Star's* coverage of: Philippe Rushton, the genetic discoveries that disprove popular notions of 'race', and its expose of racial profiling practiced by the Toronto Police Service. Through a textual analysis that combines the insights of Barthes' notion of myth (Barthes, 1972; Gaines, 2001) using tools derived from critical discourse analysis (Dellinger, 1995; Huckin, n.d.; van Dijk, 1998, 2001, 2002), this research reveals that a conservative racialized discourse lies beneath *The Star's* seemingly critical stance on issues of racism. Indeed, although the *Toronto Star's* coverage of aforementioned issues appears, ostensibly, to be critical of racism it, nonetheless, maintains and perpetuates dominant perceptions of 'race' as both an arbitrary social construct and as a construct that exists in and through language (Appiah, 1995; Hall, 1995; Pieterse, 1995).

Deconstructing the language of 'race', using Barthes' concept of myth through tools derived from critical discourse analysis (CDA), reveals the ways that 'race' has become reified as an objective, biological, reality within a popular collective consciousness. This is reflected in a common racial discourse practiced in the public sphere, represented in the media, and institutionalized through government policy. The modern concept of 'race', as a dominant cultural myth in contemporary Western society, has been naturalized through ideology and de-contextualized from the material and historical conditions of its origin in the process. As a result, 'race' has come to exist as both an imaginary social construct and as a construct that has a real material and historical impact on the populations that people are positioned by discourse as subjects within a broader colonial ideology. This ideology works through myth, obscuring the historical context of 'race' by naturalizing a language about it. Hiding the real relations of power, a colonized discourse about 'race' essentially positions people as subjects, within distinct populations, along lines of dominance and subordination. This becomes evident in the ways that difference is coded through racialized categories that have become institutionalized through the policies and ordinary discourses of a 'multicultural' society like Canada.

II. O' CANADA...OUR HOME ON NATIVE LAND?

A PARADOX OF BELONGING – The Construction of a Common Canadian

> *'What does it mean to be Canadian?' It means being willing to circulate indefinitely about an impossible object, thereby achieving the articulation of one's embodied subjectivity with the process of rational-bureaucratic domination, production and consumption that comprise a 'Canadian' life.*
> (Day, 1998, p.42)

A common, everyday discourse on cultural diversity is matched by a parallel policy on 'official multiculturalism' in Canada. This concept of 'official multiculturalism' signifies the state initiated endeavour at diffusing a national identity crisis in the face of: increasing non-European immigration from the third-world leading to increased cultural diversity; the emergent tendency towards armed struggles over land claims as seen through the American Indian Movement (AIM) among indigenous populations within the nation's borders; and the looming threat of armed struggles from Quebec militants that fuelled separatist movements in the province (Bannerji, 2000).

'Official multiculturalism' appeared as a gift that Pierre Trudeau offered an unsettled nation to disarm the radical and militant social movements that were brewing. Moreover, an official policy on multiculturalism reduced the political and economic demands of these groups to mere concerns over culture. As a result multiculturalism was used to incorporate the threat of radical social resistance within a dominant anglo-Canadian national imaginary (Bannerji, 2000). Indeed, this 'official' policy of multiculturalism came to define a nation amidst a brewing sea of political discontent. Through the process of 'orientalizing' difference (Said, 1978), diversity, from the outset, was considered to be a politically perceived public problem (Day, 1998).

> The problem of Canadian diversity has always been public, has always involved state-sponsored attempts to structure the possible field of action

> of problematic Others, and it has always been articulated with the discourse on British-Canadian *unity*. The reality of Canadian diversity is symbiotically dependent upon this will to unity – without it, diversity does not exist and certainly cannot be a problem. (Day, 1998, p.44)

Building upon the state sanctioned introduction of Canada's *Multiculturalism Policy* of 1971, The *Canadian Multiculturalism Act* was adopted by parliament in 1988. According to a Government of Canada website on Canadian Heritage, the adoption of *The Act* placed Canada on the map as the first nation to pass a law affirming a notion of 'official multiculturalism' as a principle Canadian value (Minister of State – Multiculturalism, n.d.). This value serves to define an imaginary nation through a multicultural politics, essentializing fixed cultural differences in relation to a 'Canadian culture' without regard or input from those whom the policy and *The Act* essentially subjugates (Bannerji, 2000). It is largely based on the notion that diversity must be managed in the interest of colonial superiority. Indeed, diversity only became a problem when British-Canadian sovereignty was put to the test. Furthermore, what *The Act* assumed and still assumes about immigrants is that they can be defined, classified, and fixed as such, strictly along the lines of culture and ethnicity, and loosely along the lines of 'race'.

With a policy that touts aphorisms implying a richness of difference through tolerance – as a virtuous marker of national identity – Canada is the perfect site of critical analysis to demystify a dominant 'myth about race'. In this space of tolerance and difference, the notion of diversity is essentialized within the identity politics of a Canadian multicultural imaginary. Ostensibly, Canadian identity is contingent upon the tolerance of difference through the institutionalization of an 'official multiculturalism'. In contrast to its American neighbours to the south, who invite or coerce – depending on your political predisposition – immigrants to assimilate within a homogenous national imaginary by relinquishing their original cultural norms as secondary, Canada prides its national identity on the notion that many 'varieties of people' can retain, practice, and preserve their original cultural heritage within its borders. The latter has been termed a cultural 'mosaic' whereas the former has been termed a cultural 'melting pot'. (Bannerji, 2000; Day, 1998)

TWO SIDES OF THE SAME COIN – Metaphors 'Melting Pot' and 'Mosaic'

A 'melting pot', although originally comprised of disparate parts, produces a homogenous stew whereby the distinctions between the original ingredients are no longer readily apparent. A 'mosaic', however, describes a national imaginary that is essentially comprised of the sum of its disparate parts. Essential to the composition of a 'mosaic' is the assumption that it retains the original qualities of the individual parts that comprise it as a whole. This further implies that the essence of its composite parts remains intact and is easily distinguishable from the other parts that are included within the overall national picture. Where the 'melting pot' metaphor has been perceivably marked by a process of assimilation, the 'mosaic' metaphor has been perceivably marked by a process of integration.

Richard Day (1998) assesses the definitions of assimilation and integration as two main approaches to dealing with diversity. According to Day (1998), the traditional definitions of these two terms are presented as binary opposites. Assimilation is what integration is not, and vice versa. Where assimilation calls for the abandonment of distinctive group traits in the interest of the dominant imaginary, Integration is supposed to accommodate diverse groups as they retain their distinct, defining qualities, participating equally within the overall social imaginary. A paradox is created by virtue of the definition of the latter process. If distinct groups are to retain the qualities that make them distinct, how are they to participate equally in the overall social imaginary? According to Day (1998), this problem offers an easy solution under assimilation.

Under assimilation, distinct groups give up the qualities that define them by undergoing a transformation from a state of "otherness" to a state of "sameness" (Day, 1998, p. 57). Under integration, however, distinct groups are expected to retain their 'otherness' while assuming an overall quality of 'sameness'. This outlines the impossibility of 'official multiculturalism' as the defining image of a unified Canadian identity. Day (1998) sums up this paradox quite elegantly by stating that "as the Canadian National Thing, the Mosaic functions as the object of a desire for a Canadian identity that forever fails to achieve its goal, and thereby achieves its aim, which is to perpetuate itself" (p. 43). This is not to say, however, that the 'melting pot' metaphor is better suited towards defining a national identity over the 'mosaic' metaphor.

It is important at this juncture to state that I am not advocating one metaphor (melting pot vs. mosaic) over the other, nor am I pushing for one process (assimilation vs. integration) as the ideal model towards dealing with diversity[9]. Both metaphors and processes essentially strive towards the same ends by nuanced and overlapping methods. Attempts to attain homogeneity may be attained through overt coercion as well as through

---

9 While delivering a paper at the University of Montreal on February 24th 2005, at 7th Colloquium of the CEETUM for Students and New Researchers, I was asked what approach to dealing with diversity I think to be more correct; the 'melting pot' or the 'mosaic'. I was unaware that by discussing both approaches, while concentrating my criticism on one, that I may have inadvertently appeared to be championing one metaphor over the other. To clarify my position with respect to understanding the structurally racist ties intrinsic to both methods of managing difference, I had only intended to use both metaphors for the purpose of highlighting the differences in the quality of racism between Canada and the United States. It is important to note that however different the quality of racism may be between these two countries, they share a common structural root that, in opinion, is both imperialistic and Eurocentric at its core.

forms subtle seduction in both models and approaches. Indeed, both models and approaches ultimately continue the legacy of imperialistic goals in the exploitation and subjugation of 'otherness' through the domination of imagined differences by virtue of an imagined 'sameness'. For the purpose of this thesis, however, I will be concentrating on the latter approach to dealing with diversity; the cultural mosaic as it applies to 'official multiculturalism' in the constitution of a 'Canadian identity'. As seductive or coercive as the 'mosaic' may appear, it holds unto itself its own sets of myths containing ideologies that obscure the power relations at work among its disparate parts.

An official policy of multiculturalism solidifies and shapes the cultural 'mosaic' metaphor. Where the parts that make up the 'mosaic' translate into 'varieties of people' within the Canadian cultural landscape, the entire 'mosaic' comes to represent the overall Canadian cultural imaginary as a variety of cultures interpreted officially as *multicultural*. In theory, multiculturalism allows the harmonious intermixing of different cultures to be *tolerated* within the overall national imaginary. Tolerance, however, does not necessitate acceptance. As a result, inclusiveness is merely tolerated on the surface.

A concept of Diversity that includes reified notions of 'race' becomes a buzzword signifying a sort of *multi-cultural* ornamentation, conveniently used to decorate an imagined national identity[10]. This is done without allowing equal access for those 'varieties of people', defined as culturally different from those whose power defines them, to participate equally in the shaping of the national identity. This creates a notion of tolerance that obscures struggles towards justice and equality and masks oppression under a guise of privilege. As a result, it becomes assumed – by virtue of a perceived

---

[10] For more details on an 'imagined national identity' in the Canadian context, please see Tony Wilden's *The Imaginary Canadian* (1980).

attitude of imperial arrogance – that immigrants should be viewed as privileged enough to be allowed to integrate into a 'Canadian society', despite their subsequent marginalization and civic annihilation regarding any social, political, and economic input as to what should constitute a 'Canadian society'. Their civic prowess becomes castrated while the potential power of their presence is rendered impotent with regards to contributing to the shape of the Canadian imaginary through the official mechanisms of integration/ assimilation.

Immigrants, especially those of colour (a designation of 'racial' difference), are to be considered privileged as citizens under the civilizing project of Canadian multiculturalism. Difference is tolerated so long as it can eventually conform to the ideal European imaginary that has colonized and 'fathered' the imaginary that we have come to know as Canada. As a result, racism continues to exist surreptitiously within the institutional fabric of a 'multicultural' Canadian society. What this model fails to realize in theory, however, has manifested itself within the strict reality of racist practices carried out by the institutions designed to accommodate its parts (varieties of people). Missing from the 'mosaic' analogy is the fluid quality of culture and its evolutionary propensity for change and development.

III. LOCATING CULTURE IN MULTICULTURE

PERPETUALLY RECEDING HORIZONS – Constructing Cultural Imaginings

> *Philosophically, I do not believe in the purity of cultures, or even in the possibility of identifying them as meaningfully discrete wholes. I think of cultures as complex human practices of signification and representation, of organization and attribution, which are internally riven by conflicting narratives. Cultures are formed through complex dialogues with other cultures. In most cultures that have attained some degree of internal differentiation, the dialogue of the other(s) is internal rather than intrinsic to the culture itself.* (Benhabib, 2002, p. ix)

According to Seyla Benhabib (2002), what we come to know and classify as distinct cultures have become "badges of identity" through the faulty epistemic premises of what she terms the "reductionist sociology of culture" (p. 4). For Benhabib (2002), conservatives and progressives alike base their perceptions of culture on the assumption that: they are "clearly delineable wholes"; they can be applied as uncontroversial classificatory labels to population groups; and the hybridity and overlap of population groups ascribed to more than one culture does not pose a problem for policy (p. 4). Based on these faulty epistemic premises, policies like the *Canadian Multiculturalism Act* have been institutionalized to reify, essentialize, fetishize, naturalize, and organize difference within a public multicultural discourse. It is important, however, not to take this perception of culture at face value. More attention must be paid to a critical analysis of the structure imbedded in the composition of this multicultural discourse.

Using a "narrative view of actions and culture", Benhabib (2002) peels back the layers of the essentialized cultural perspective used by the "reductionist sociology of culture" (pp. 4-5). The starting point for analysis is to differentiate the subject/ object relationship between the perspective of 'social observer' and the 'social agent' with regards to the analyzed cultural entity. According to Benhabib (2002), the "social observer...is one who imposes, together with local elites, unity and coherence on cultures as observed entities" whereas 'social agents' – in contrast, participants in culture – "experience their traditions, stories, rituals and symbols, tools and material living conditions through shared, albeit contested and contestable, narrative accounts" (p. 5). This distinction is important in its implications that the former, 'social observer' must essentially view cultures as distinct wholes for the purposes of coherence, classification and control. This standpoint can only be assessed and imposed from the 'outside'. In contrast, the latter – 'social agent' – does not need to view what they agree their culture to be as a whole because their standpoint is experienced from the 'inside'.

The 'social agent' perspective is a rather telling one, with regards to the structure of cultural construction, primarily because cultures are formed through contested accounts. According to Benhabib (2002), this is evident for two reasons. The first reason is illustrated through a 'double hermeneutic'. This implies that "we identify *what* we do through an *account* of what we do" (Benhabib, 2002, p. 6). Indeed, meaning in all socially significant action is determined through communication. As a result, action(s) gain significance through the accounts of the agent as well as others in reference to the action(s) performed. This locates culture as a social entity constituted within webs of overlapping and contested narratives.

The second reason that cultures are formed through contested accounts refers to an evaluative dimension of actions. Benhabib (2002) considers this evaluative dimension to be a "second-order narrative" (p. 7). This second-order narrative implies a 'normative attitude' towards first-order accounts of actions about narratives. For Benhabib (2002), these 'normative attitudes' derived from an evaluative dimension form the basis of cultures. Because there are two dimensions of contested accounts – two levels of narrative contestation – cultures cannot be fixed as delineable wholes. They are constantly shifting entities that "form a horizon that recedes each time one approaches it" (Benhabib, 2002, p. 5). This has very salient implications when applied to notions of multiculturalism.

MULTICULTURALISM AND THE CONFINEMENT OF CULTURE

Notions of 'official multiculturalism' are based on the faulty premises of the 'reductionist sociology of culture' (Benhabib, 2002). This perspective, further assumes that cultures can be preserved. Because cultures are not the fixed, delineable parts that can be frozen in time to comprise a completed national picture, "culture is not something that can be preserved nor conserved" (Walcott, 2003, p. 139). Following the logic of this premise, if cultures cannot be preserved or conserved because they do not exist as delineable wholes – due to the fact that their form is constituted in contested narratives – then they cannot properly fit as parts within a multicultural mosaic. A multicultural 'mosaic', therefore, cannot sufficiently serve as a proper metaphor that identifies and defines a complete and inclusive national portrait. Subscribing to a belief on the contrary is problematic on two levels.

First, to assume the possibility of a complete national portrait would be to finalize the national identity as frozen within time. So doing would essentially position the national identity as transcendent to its social and historical context. This would eliminate the possibility for change via growth and development. As a result, the national image, as it currently exists, could only be interpreted as a-historical. This would mean that it has always naturally existed as it is, in its current conception, and it will remain so forever. Furthermore, the naturalization of an a-historical national identity would ultimately exclude immigrant input as alien from 'without', while being antithetical to difference from 'within'. To clarify this point, immigrants could not integrate within the national imaginary without first being cleansed of the qualities that make them different in relation to those who constitute the national imaginary. Those qualities are essentially what constitute their difference as immigrants. As a result, difference cannot be fully accepted within the national imaginary because the national imaginary ultimately strives towards homogeneity which is actually antithetical to the very notion of difference that immigrant populations represent. These immigrant populations are considered to be necessary ornaments within a multicultural 'mosaic'. Without them, the 'mosaic' could not exist. For immigrants to occupy space within the national imaginary as immigrants (those defined in difference to the national status quo) their input must be viewed as alien to the homogeneity that has already been achieved through consensus *a priori* within the imaginary itself (exclusively formed by a dominant colonizing force).

As diversity becomes homogenized under the rubric of the national imaginary, difference (in the 'liberal' sense) can only be tolerated and not fully accepted, if this national imaginary is in fact antithetical to the very notion of difference. Despite this logic, however, the Canadian identity – as comprised within a multicultural 'mosaic' – continues to be premised on a static concept of culture that has become naturalized through myth within the national imaginary. (Bannerji, 2000; Bissoondath, 2002; Walcott, 2003)

The second level, where imagining cultures as fixed wholes within the national image constitutes a problem, can be seen in the current disposition of the various cultures that form the surface of this national portrait. Because difference cannot be fully accepted, these diverse cultures are seen as naturally located outside of the national imaginary despite the fact that they reside within its composition. The centre/ periphery image created in the relationships of cultural and economic class holds true in this sense as difference is pushed out towards the margins in order to be better managed by the colonizing interior. Furthermore, given the problems of locating diversity within the national imaginary, an 'official multicultural mosaic' as constitutive of the Canadian identity is problematic in the way in which it fixes the diverse cultural parts as manageable objects.

DEHUMANIZING OBJECTS OF DIFFERENCE AND A CULT OF FETISH

Although the location of diverse cultures appears to exist naturally on the periphery, objectified through the 'impressive ideological formations' of imperialism as manageable commodities, they are in fact constituted and positioned that way by the dominant forces that define them as such. Edward Said (1978) eloquently captures this sentiment when he states that "only the Orientalist can interpret the Orient, the Orient being radically incapable of interpreting itself" (p. 289). Because of this, the limited perception of the 'social observer' (Benhabib, 2002) is driven by the need to essentialize a fixed cultural badge to the object of difference being managed. This fixed cultural badge becomes worn like a straightjacket to keep difference confined within the trivialities of their subjugated positioning. The diverse cultures that make up the portrait of Canada, therefore, are narrowly reduced to one-dimensional caricatures, commodified by the fruits of their 'exotic' lifestyles.

Material products like food, costume, and music are cultural artefacts that can be packaged, marketed, and sold to consumers to concretize an imagined multicultural national identity. These cultural parts are themselves fractured pieces of broader, fluid, cultural heritages that are now reduced to the aesthetic shells of consumption by the dominant Canadian imaginary. Seen as nothing more than an aesthetic appeal to the 'exotic', these cultural fragments adorn the Canadian imaginary like ornaments: visible, manageable, trinkets of convenience. In the process of fragmenting identity, the producers of commodified cultural artefacts become objectified themselves. This objectification of difference is a patently dehumanizing act of power exercised in the interests of the dominant group.

According to Paulo Freire (1970), the act of dehumanization is a crucial marker of oppression played out in the dialectical relationship between a dominant class and a subordinated class – both of which can only exist in relation to one another. For Freire (1970), "an act is oppressive only when it prevents men [*sic*] from being more fully human" (p. 42). The objectification of difference is one such act that is executed by the dominant or oppressive class through the exclusive conception of themselves as human beings. To clarify this point, one must remember that the notion of 'self' – the dominant 'oppressors' – is solely contingent on the definition 'other' – the 'oppressed' class. This definition of 'other', therefore, is not only different from the notion of 'self' but as signifiers of identity they are diametrically opposed. For 'self' to lay exclusive claim to the status of humanity, 'other' – by default – must be dehumanized in the interest of maintaining one's humanity solely at the expense of another's. This is further illustrated by the dominant class' belief that everything – including other people – can be objectified as commodities to be managed and purchased. Difference, in this case must necessarily be objectified and ultimately dehumanized in order for the dominant class to maintain its privileged position of power.

> It could not be otherwise. If the humanization of the oppressed signifies subversion, so also does their freedom; hence the necessity for constant control. And the more the oppressors control the oppressed, the more they change them into apparently inanimate "things." (Freire, 1970, p. 45)

Difference, therefore, is not *accepted*, but merely *tolerated* as an act of imperial arrogance. Under this arrogance, reinforced by Canada's 'official multiculturalism', tolerance becomes a privilege afforded to alterity by the benevolence of Empire. Accommodating diversity exclusively on a superficial level, so long as the national imaginary remains the product of its colonial founders, Canada's 'official multiculturalism' segregates its citizens, constituting a form of cultural apartheid. Alienated from the national imaginary, cultural differences become reduced as objectified ornaments of diverse fetishes.

Fetishizing cultural difference allows for the inclusion and spectacle of ornamentation (via cultural artefacts or objectified others), while excluding the people that produce these artefacts as *real* citizens within the Canadian imaginary. Reducing perceived cultures to random, fragmented aspects of their hybrid and evolving lifestyles, essentially robs the members of these perceived cultures of their potential to participate as equal citizens that make up the country. For example, to the 'social observer' Chinese culture becomes narrowly defined by perceived foods and festivals, patronizingly and generically referred to as *Chinese*. The same can be seen with respect to almost all other ethnic groups and perceived cultural wholes that are constituted within the 'mosaic'. In this superficial instance, the visuospatial metaphor of centre and periphery appears to dissolve under the rubric of the 'mosaic' metaphor, ostensibly implying a sense of progress towards the 'liberal' notion of equality.

MULTICULTURAL MOSAIC – Centre & Periphery Reborn in the 'Ex-factor'

Within the 'mosaic' metaphor, the *centre* is perceived to be subsumed by the *periphery*. As a result, the illusion of a unified, homogeneous whole is created even though it is actually constituted thoroughly by various fluid, heterogeneous parts. This occurs primarily due to the fact that a dominant group – characterized within a racialized hierarchy by a value of 'whiteness'[11] – has been written out of the metaphor, as an invisible, ubiquitous and creative force that enables the 'mosaic' to exist. Indeed, the 'mosaic' is a product of the dominant group's creative imagination. As the dominant group, impelled by the 'impressive ideological formations' of imperial designs, remains 'ex-nominated' (Barthes, 1972, 1984) in the 'mosaic', the metaphor becomes solidified and secured. 'Whiteness', therefore, serves as a 'normative' value in relation to the mosaic and is rendered invisible. This invisibility allows 'whiteness' as a normative value to remain 'unnamed'. Borrowing Barthes' (1972, 1984) concept of denomination, the power dynamic intrinsic to the precarious positioning of unnamed engineers of the 'mosaic' is precisely what I would refer to as the 'ex-factor'. Power, in this sense, operates by separating the *creator* and the object *created* at safe distances from each other

---

11 According to Ruth Frankenberg (1993), 'whiteness' is structured within a negotiated terrain of historical and material contingencies. Like other racialized constructs – such as 'blackness' – 'whiteness' exists as a means of articulating lived experiences through 'race' and is by no means a monolithic entity. Indeed, people who are perceived as 'white' are also racialized and exhibit many ways of living 'whiteness'. Exploring and naming 'whiteness', attempts at demystifying its apparent normative and invisible qualities with respect to the perceived racial neutrality about it. This perceived racial neutrality is part and parcel an effect of its dominance where subjects are positioned within social, political, and economic relations of power. The meanings generated about these relations that help to define the positions of social actors (subjects) situated within them, are socially constructed and are, therefore, susceptible to shift over time and are in no way absolute. As a result, 'whiteness' can be interpreted as a relational category, defined in 'racisms' that determine other racialized categories. For the purpose of this thesis, however, "the term 'whiteness' signals the production and reproduction of dominance rather than subordination, normativity rather than marginality, and privilege rather than disadvantage" (Frankenberg, 1993, pp. 236-237).

discursively. This becomes evident, for example, when examining government census data on diversity.

According to the 2001 Census Highlights, produced by the Ontario Ministry of Finance, the province of Ontario appears to be increasingly diverse (see Appendix A). As a result, it can be said that Ontario is becoming increasingly *multicultural*. If Ontario is perceived as becoming increasingly 'multicultural', Canada – by default – is also seen as becoming increasingly 'multicultural' since Ontario is a province of Canada (Census 2001 Highlights). Accompanied by an array of colourful charts, a graph, and statistics, is the subheading "Visible Minorities Making Canada Increasingly Diverse." This subheading anchors the statistics that purportedly point to increased diversity without truly defining what is meant by diversity. Interestingly enough, however, 'visible minorities' are defined "as persons, other than Aboriginal peoples, who are non-Caucasian in race or non-white in colour." 'White' becomes the base signifier from which all difference is measured. Caucasian is the 'race' – based on a flawed taxonomy – that tenuously connects false notions of racial designation to narrowly defined notions of fixed cultures while remaining invisible beyond the scope of difference.

'Whiteness', characterized by subscription to a Western ideology, as a broad classification of a dominant racialized group, is known in reference to everything that it is not. To explain this further, there are no cultural ornaments that straightjacket a 'white' cultural horizon as a delineable whole. 'White', as it appears to exist in binary opposition to that which it has narrowly defined as "other" or 'coloured' is actually based on a hierarchical relationship. This is what Edward Said (1993) refers to when he states that cultural identities are not essentializations that exist as complete entities in nature – even though the essentializations of cultural identities are considered to be part of their "enduring appeal" – but are in fact "contrapuntal ensembles" formed in an array of "opposites" and "negatives" (p. 52). Cultural identity, therefore, is formed within a sea of 'contested narratives' (Benhabib, 2002) that contributes to the essence of its hybridity. It becomes problematic to fair and equal social relations, when one group dominates through the realization its own hybridity by denying the hybrid quality of the 'other' groups that it subjugates. The hybridity of the dominant cultural entity is already assumed in its absence from the 'mosaic'. The 'mosaic', therefore, becomes a conceptual tool of dominance solely reserved to define and manage *difference* and not *sameness*.

This categorization of difference within the 'mosaic' allows for the visibility of diverse groups to be managed and policed in a surreptitiously different way than other Canadians of a less visible stature (or those whose visibility is absorbed *a priori* in the constitution of the Canadian imaginary with no fixed status of pseudo-belonging). Difference, in this case, becomes coded in relation to an idealized standard of the 'self'. As an idealized standard or centre around which difference orbits, the 'self' is defined in its 'non-differential' status. The 'self' is titled as such because it is not the 'other'. Not only is 'other' necessarily defined in difference from the 'self', 'self' also comes into existence by creating and locating 'other' in order to reduce the anxiety created by an identity crisis (Eze, 2001; Fanon, 1967). The identity of the 'self' is contingent upon the clarity of difference agreed upon through convention in the production and process of positioning 'other' in relation to what the 'self' believes it is not. 'Self' and 'other' are hierarchical subjects in a performative play of relational difference.

> The construction of identity – for identity…while obviously a repository of distinct collective experiences, is finally a construction in my opinion – involves the construction of opposites and "others" whose actuality is

> always subject to the continuous interpretation and re-interpretation of their differences from "us"...Far from a static thing then, identity of self or "other" is a much worked over historical, social, intellectual, and political process that takes place as a contest involving individuals and institutions in all societies. (Said, 1978, p.332)

Intrinsic to this process, 'self' maintains a position of privilege by virtue of its exclusive access to shaping the national imaginary and its subsequent right to establish boundaries of membership by naming difference. Indeed, the 'impressive ideological formations' that fashion and drive imperialism has imbued those positioned as 'self' with the power to represent and speak for those they position as 'other'. This relationship, perpetuated by unlimited access to the national imaginary, is legitimated through myths that serve to enforce and preserve a current balance of power in society. These myths work to maintain privilege for the position of 'self' through the imperialistic ideologies of racism as they become naturalized by the consensus of the dominant class.

Since notions of 'other' are different from 'self', and it is precisely this difference that necessitates the existence of the 'self', myth is used to naturalize these differences creating the least amount of potential for possible resistance. Although gaps are inherently created by difference, as it is systematically coded by the ideologies of the privileged class positioned as 'self', myth is used to employ ideologies that work to smooth out the gaps and potential class conflicts coded through difference. In other words, myth serves to obfuscate the social relations of power – as seen through the ways in which racialized communities are constituted in the social organization of classes – that order perceived cultural differences making them appear natural.

By segregating naturally perceived cultural differences, the formation of potential networked solidarities are discouraged, creating the impression that coalition building is an impossible feat based on the illusion of the incommensurability and incompatibility of diverse cultural communities. As a result, various racialized communities are placed in a relative state of competitiveness with one another; further obscuring any commonalities that they may share through the historical and material conditions that constitute class distinctions (Bannerji, 2000). According to Bannerji (2000), "a concept of class helps us to see the network of social relations constituting an overall social organization which both implicates and cuts through racialization/ ethnicization and gender" (p. 7).

Once class relations are obscured in the mythic constructions of racialized and cultured communities, difference of the 'other' must be tolerated in order for 'other' to be positioned as subordinate while creating an environment with the least potential for resistance. By positioning 'other' as a cultural fetish to be consumed at a moment's convenience, the growth and development of cultures are ultimately restricted. The Canadian policy of 'official multiculturalism' is one way in which the gap of difference is smoothed over using the 'liberal' ideology of tolerance. This limits the scope and depth of Canadian cultural identities and ultimately, intentional or not, sanctions racial hierarchies as naturalized within the myth about 'race'.

Despite the current rhetoric of tolerance, 'official multiculturalism' serves to further perpetuate a notion of exclusion that has very insidious effects on the social relations of citizens within the national composition. Based on this 'liberal' rhetoric of tolerance, ultimately alienating cultures through marked exclusion from the national imaginary, 'official multiculturalism' has set a precedent for the practices of racism that plagues the lives of various Canadian communities. Inspiring a normalizing discourse of 'acceptable' oppression through the practice of racial profiling by police services like Toronto, and the subsequent coding of racialized difference in the 'liberal' media, the perceived notion of 'race' as scripted within 'official multiculturalism', must be explored and deconstructed as a signifier constructed in and through language.

IV. HISTORICAL CONTINGENCIES TO RACIALIZED REALITIES

LANGUAGE OF RELATIONAL DIFFERENCES – 'Race' of Ancients to Irish

> *And the mind that has conceived a plan of living must never loose sight of the chaos against which that pattern was conceived [...] Thus, having tried to give pattern to the chaos which lives within the patterns of your certainties, I must come out, I must emerge.*
> (Ellison, 1947, pp. 580-581)

The construction of 'race' through language reveals one of the biggest illusions of Western civilization. In contrast to common perceptions about it, 'race' is not a bio-genetic reality. Traditional notions of 'race' as seen through somatic differences, based on skin colour and hair texture, come from Western myths of objective realism that inform a dominant world view. Grounded in the dominant notion of reality, 'race' remains an unrelenting part of some of the most oppressive ideologies (Hall, 1995). Like perceived notions of reality, the material assumptions about 'race' are subject to critical discursive analysis.

Throughout history 'race' has become a way of classifying people of the world into groups of relational differences. Constituted in language, these values in difference have changed among and between civilizations, over time. Such classifications of distinct populations are formulated in systems of difference that are socially and historically contingent. These systems of difference are motivated by discourses that form the distinct realities of separate world views. Because of these factors, ways of ordering existence in relation to 'others' can be interpreted as arbitrary constructions even though they constitute common social knowledge through myth. This is seen in the ways past civilizations have ordered their realm in terms of racial differences.

Kwame Anthony Appiah (1995) offers a brief historiography on the social construction of 'race'. For Appiah (1995), modern racial categories are seen as ideological constructs contingent upon the varied histories of different civilizations. These constructs are subject manifestations of dominant conceptual frameworks or myth. As ideological creations, they become susceptible to the shifting climate of their respective historical and material conditions that temper a relative social atmosphere. For example, one way that people delineated perceived racial difference was through common subscriptions to religious beliefs and practices. This is seen in the ways in which the ancient Greeks and Hebrews distinguished themselves as separate from other populations that they had encountered.

Delineating themselves as different from the rest of the world, the ancient Hebrews culturally located each other in allegiance to the same God. Everyone who worshiped the same God, in the same manner, was considered members of the same 'race' (Appiah, 1995). Essentially those claiming membership to the same 'race' were assumed to be subscribing to the same world view. In so doing, each individual lived within the dominant framework of a shared reality. Although the ancient Hebrews had one way of interpreting their existence by classifying difference, *theocentric* myths were not the only form of ordering the ancient world.

In ancient Greece, the Hellenes distinguished themselves from the rest of the world according to the environment in which they lived. In the fifth century B.C, Hippocrates believed his 'race' to be naturally tougher and more independent than the people of Asia Minor in the West (Appiah, 1995). His belief was largely based on the perceivably unique environmental conditions through which the population that he belonged to developed and thrived. His reasoning behind this was that the infertile soils had forced them to evolve that way. 'Race' is distinguished here, not in terms of theological affiliation, but in terms of geographical *logos* and personal worth. Above all, this notion of personal worth was based less on biology and more so determined by "the nature of the political relationship between peoples which causes a people to be viewed in a particular light" (Pieterse, 1995, p. 26). Following this line of reasoning it becomes clear that the concept of 'race' has not always been confined exclusively to a biological explanation.

Jan Nederveen Pieterse (1995) argues that the concept of 'race' is not biologically grounded at all. As an ideologically loaded construct, the modern assumption about 'race', as a valid biological taxonomy, is in fact a socio-political fabrication. Pieterse (1995) examines the ways in which 'race' and class intersect through systems of domination. Indeed, both of these forms of social stratification are inextricably linked through specific histories, ideologies, and the underlying logic of how power in society is distributed (Pieterse, 1995). Although power in society was in some cases defined and exercised through class relations it was also defined and exercised in part by differences in physical appearances as a result of the imperial conquests of 'other' civilizations like those in Africa.

Throughout modern history, where there has been an unequal distribution of power in society, people who have been subjugated to the powers of dominant groups have been compared to dark skinned Africans either in terms of status, treatment, or appearance (Pieterse, 1995). For example, Chamfort, during the 18th century, referred to the poor underclass as the Negroes of Europe (Pieterse, 1995). In this case class distinctions were coded as racial difference. Although 'race' was also coded on the basis of somatic features – as seen in the ways that the British colonizers referred to East

Indians as *niggers* on the basis of skin colour – 'race' was not always exclusive to biological interpretation. 'Race' – as a way of delineating differences between populations – was primarily a way of politically justifying an Empire's moral right to subject conquered populations to powers of domination (Said, 1978, 1993). As an imperialistic discourse, the concept of 'race' was even used in the British treatment of the Irish.

Shortly after the Anglo-Norman invasions, the Irish were considered to be a savage and barbaric 'race' of people. They were seen, by the British, uncivilized, just like the rebellious tribes of Africa and the America's. From the 19th century forward, the British began to depict the Irish as sharing some of the same physical traits that were supposedly exclusive to Negroes in various printed illustrations and cartoons. The Irish were looked upon as having darker skin than the average Caucasian and were characterized as exhibiting ape-like features in many publications and illustrations of the time. They were *White Negroes* (Pietrerse, 1995). This phenomenon was further compounded by the sudden influx of Irish immigrants during the famine of 1840, and their constant resistance to British rule. The title 'white negroes', however, did not remain a fixed category in which all Irish would be classified. The Irish were eventually able to assimilate into 'whiteness' (Postal & Ignatiev, 1997) by identifying with other Europeans through somatic features[12]. A racialized caste system based on somatic

---

[12] American history has recorded incidents of European bond-labourers on perceivably equal footing with their African counterparts especially during the 17th century. Both groups were initially united by their membership in a shared working class and would find solidarity in various revolts and uprisings. In order to curb this solidarity to weaken revolts, new forms of solidarity were organized, produced and reproduced along notions of 'race'. These new forms of solidarity were based on skin colour, bringing about a new form of social control in the 'invention of the white race'. For more information on this transition see Theodore W. Allen's (1994) *The Invention of the White Race: The Origins of Racial Oppression in Anglo America*.

differences that created a hierarchical structure for ordering 'races' was also initiated from the outset of Western and capitalist imperial expansion.

EMPIRE AND THE BIRTH OF 'RACE' AS A BIOLOGICAL TAXOMOMY

As Western empires expanded, under capitalist and imperial endeavours, their populations became exposed to other populations that looked 'exotic' them. This discovery created anxieties among Western populations – including the poor and the Irish – that led to a crisis of identity. Practicing new customs, the 'exotic' beings stood outside of any previously held identity profile. Indeed, they were even considered beneath Europe's poor. They had dark skin – even darker than the poor and the Irish – and were considered to be direct opposites of the Europeans. A new system of categorizing individuals into groups was devised to soothe the anxieties caused by the identity crisis felt by the colonizers.

Colonizers believed that one way of categorizing everyone, was through 'sensible' somatic differences. Seeing that these strange beings had features like dark skin and coarsely textured hair – in contrast to the skin and hair of the colonizers – somatic distinctions appeared to be a logical way of coding difference. Difference, in this capacity, was quickly appropriated within a dominant biological discourse used to distinguish the colonized from the colonizers. These features became naturalized demarcations of racial identity. As a result, 'race', was, and in some cases still remains, biologically defined as a natural way of categorizing differences among people. In order to illustrate this continuity in racism, from ancient societies through imperial colonialism to present, one must carefully examine the 'peculiar institutions' (Wacquant, 2002) that continually produce new 'racisms' while attempting to maintain fixed notions of 'race' (Hall, 1995, 1996, 1997, 2002).

'PECULIAR INSTITUTIONS' AND THE PRODUCTION OF RACISMS

Loic Wacquant (2002) identifies the ways in which 'racisms' have been perpetuated throughout American history as the result of the development of at least four main 'peculiar institutions' that helped to define the social relations of power in American society. These four main institutions – chattel slavery and restricted labour, the Jim Crow system of legalized segregation, the ghettoization of urban living spaces, and the penal system of mass incarceration – all contributed to the legitimization, normalization, and perpetuation of everyday 'racisms'. The existence of 'racisms' that emerge as a result of these institutions are defined in the specific social relations of power that operate to position, manage, and control populations of 'other' (most noticeably peoples of the African diasporas currently labelled 'black') (Podur, 2002; Wacquant, 2002).

Here we can clearly see the historical link between the 'strange fruit' of the colonial past and the 'strange fruit' of the 'tolerant' present. What is of particular importance to this thesis, drawing from this sense of historical racial continuity, is the fact that racisms emerged and continue to persist as by-products of the systemic structures of society's 'peculiar institutions'. For example, slaves were not stolen from Africa simply as a means to satisfy racist endeavours. Slaves were initially brought to the America's from Africa for their labour. Racism was produced as an effect of the dehumanizing aspects of slavery.

Slavery, as an institution that exploited the labour of objectified beings for capitalistic gain, was in dire need of a system that justified the dehumanizing aspects of its practice (Wacquant, 2002). Such a system was perceived as naturally derived from the division of labour based in the conception of racial categories. These racial categories, coupled with a disparate market economy, reinforced a racialized caste system of hierarchical ordering. This caste system was based on the creation and implementation of delineable racial categories that were devised in relation to somatic features like skin colour. Racism, therefore, was a not a precondition of slavery but a consequence. Indeed, racism actually occurred through the justification of an exploitative 'peculiar institution' in the creation and implementation of a racialized caste system. In order for the caste to work, it had to appear natural and absolute. Difference had to be marked and fixed in order to be effectively managed and dealt with. Not far removed from its roots as a construct within the market system, skin colour remains a primary signifier of difference – as previously discussed in the Census 2001 Highlights – even within a 'liberal' society that purports to tolerate diversity.

Although 'race' – commonly perceived through colour today – was born a construct, it continues to be a dominant defining quality of difference that remains couched in a myth of naturalized orientation. Despite the fact that it is an abstraction, 'race' continues to serve as an objectified social genre that is commonly used to define, categorize, separate and control groups of people. Once separated, difference can be exploited and controlled more efficiently. Because the imagined existence of separate groups – known as 'races' – have been reinforced in many ways, through various 'peculiar institutions' over time, notions of difference have become taken-for-granted, constituting a dominant social myth about 'race'.

As myth, the social, political, and historical context of 'race' has been removed from the dominant discourse about it, allowing it to exist ensconced in nature as an autonomous entity, affecting real material and historical conditions of oppression. As a result, there has been the development of some critical schools of thought that places unwarranted emphasis on the concept of 'race' as a means within itself that can purportedly be useful in organizing anti-racist practices towards social change.

PUTTING THE 'CRITICAL' BACK IN CRITICAL RACE THEORIES

Despite the fact that many forms of domination and oppression – like those based on systems of 'race', 'class', and 'gender' – are intimately connected (Hooks, 1995, 1997), there have been attempts lately by some critical 'race' theorists to forge a critical pedagogy that decentres notions of class in the interests of centring notions of 'race' (Allen, 2004; Leonardo, 2004; Lynn, 2004; Parker & Stovall, 2004). Even though their best efforts are guided by noble purposes, this centralized notion of 'race' is a curious undertaking, to say the least, especially when systems of domination and oppression are not mutually exclusive and autonomous in relation to one another. For Gregory Meyerson (2002), "oppression is multiple and intersecting but its causes are not ... it does not follow that multiple oppressions require multiple structural causes".

Modalities like gender and 'race' are forms of social stratification that are epiphenomenal attributes of a class based society (San Juan, 2002, 2003). For example, it becomes very difficult for a person to address issues of racism without exploring its connections to the globalized forms of capitalism that contribute to conditions of apartheid world wide (Marable, 2004). For this reason, some other critical theorists cannot avoid noticing the importance of class when criticizing racism as systematic phenomena (Bannerji, 2000; Cox, 1959; Darder & Torres, 2004; Meyerson, 2000; Sahay, 1998; San Juan, 2002, 2003; Scatamburlo D'Annibale & McLaren, 2003, 2004). For these theorists, class is not simply one aspect of identity but a socializing totality marked by the mechanisms of capitalism (San Juan, 2002, 2003). Based on this premise, 'racisms' are examined in the ways in which they become produced and reproduced in class-based society (Cabusao, 2005). By de-emphasizing class through an emphasis on 'race', some of the self proclaimed critical 'race' theorists essentially fix notions of 'race' as an autonomous category through which racial oppression must be exclusively handled. This only further contributes to the same acts of fetishizing and reifying 'race' that helps in maintaining the existence of the 'racisms' they purport to be stridently against (Bell, 2002; Gilroy, 2002; Sahay, 1998). This occurs despite widespread scholarly acknowledgment of the fact that 'race' is a social construct.

Even though all critical theorists will agree that 'race' is a social construct, some scholars insist on objectifying and fetishizing its abstraction, by claiming that it creates systems and circumstances for historical and material oppression. The effects of these systems and circumstances have been referred to as racism. What occurs is the proverbial 'chicken and egg' scenario. For such theorists, racism is perceived to be the natural product of distinct 'races'. Because of this they believe that 'race' must play a central role in critical theory. A contradiction exists, however, in this assessment. 'Race' as a social construct cannot produce natural phenomena; it can only produce constructs that are further removed from a historical and material base. Because of this, 'race' is not a useful analytical or discursive construct for effecting change.

As stated at the outset of this thesis, racism produces 'races' and not vice versa (Darder & Torres, 2004). By virtue of this premise, 'race' cannot explain racism (Meyerson, 2000). Class division, structured historically in the rise of imperial capitalism, produces the material circumstances that breed racism (Bohmer, n.d.; Daniels,

1996; Wacquant, 2002). The historical and material circumstances that call racism into existence, therefore, has fabricated notions of a hierarchy of distinct racialized bodies, commonly perceived as 'races'. Indeed, the existence of distinct 'races' as a biological fact is rather a science fiction composed in myth. In light of this logic, one would be more effective in the struggle against various 'racisms' by focusing less on 'race' and more on the process of 'racialization'. Even though 'race' is fictional, many people will agree that 'racialized communities' are factual, existing in the real systems and circumstances of historical and material oppression.

'RACE' vs. 'RACIALIZED COMMUNITIES' – Demystification & Emphasis

Distinguishing between notions of 'race' and 'racialized communities' is important towards the creation of a critical anti-racist discourse. The notion of 'race', as touted by pseudo-scientists like Philippe Rushton, is a biological term used for identifying subspecies (Wise, n.d.). The notion of subspecies indicates that a degree of genetic variance must be significant enough to subcategorize organisms that are on the verge of branching off into entirely new species (Wise, n.d.). This notion of 'race' further implies that the human species can be divided into subgroups as a result of naturally occurring phenomena. The term 'race' connotes a biological reality and its use is therefore problematic when articulating a constructed quality about it. Instead of using 'race' as an analytic and discursive construct, the process of racialization – through which such a construct comes into existence – may be a more useful tool of critical articulation.

According to Manning Marable (2004), 'racialization' connotes "the construction of racially unequal social hierarchies characterized by dominant and subordinate social relations between groups". For Marable (2004), this process is a global problem that is intimately connected to the rise of global capitalism – as a ubiquitous colonizing force – that causes social relationships characterized by a type of global apartheid. Apartheid is an Afrikaans word meaning separateness that is based on the concept that a 'herrenvolk' or 'master race' is destined to rule over other 'races' (Marable, 2004). Although apartheid has historically defined the white minority rule in South Africa, it should not be considered a phenomenon exclusive to racism in South Africa.

According to Marable (2004), global apartheid is "the racialized division and stratification of resources, wealth, and power that separates Europe, North America and Japan from the billions of mostly black, brown, indigenous, undocumented immigrant and poor people across the planet". For the purposes of this thesis, however, the concept of apartheid and a 'master race' can be translated into the 'strange fruit' that poison contemporary society through the racist policies and institutions of 'official multiculturalism' in Canada. As an overarching, state sanctioned discourse, 'official multiculturalism' taps into the deep structures of systemic racism that not only naturalizes the practice of racial profiling but also fuels the mass media – as yet another 'peculiar institution' – that perpetuates the myth that separate 'races' exist naturally.

THE NATURE OF THINGS – Grouping Populations According to 'Race'?

As natural as 'race' may seem, there is absolutely nothing natural about it. Indeed, there are gaps and contradictions inherent to the dominant notion that distinct 'races' actually exist in nature. These gaps and contradictions become increasingly obvious as we peel back the layers of inter-textuality that constitute a dominant myth about 'race'. As a result, 'race' becomes coded, through dominant discourses about it, as a concept that exists as a part of an objective and observable reality. Taken to be a part of objective reality – as it is interpreted to exist in nature – 'race', as a fixed subject for categorizing populations, becomes canonized as a veritable knowledge claim. This claim, however, reveals two main flaws that should not be overlooked.

First, it is virtually impossible to classify every human being into categories of skin colour and hair texture. Despite this fact, popular Western myths accept three main racial classifications. Negroid - having dark skin and coarse hair; Caucasoid - having light skin and straight hair; and Mongoloid - having pale skin and shapely eyes. If Negroes have dark skin and coarse hair, and Caucasians have light skin and straight hair, where do the majority of East Indian people fit in? Most of them have dark skin and straight hair. This model of classification also serves to alienate and exclude many aboriginal groups as being void of racial distinction. After all, according to these narrow traits of classification, some aboriginal groups may fit the category of Mongoloid because of their light skin and shapely eyes; but what of those with dark skin and coarse hair?

Second, if 'race' is biological, why is it not contingent upon other biological distinctions that our species share? Why should race be divided along the lines of skin colour and hair texture? Why not eye colour and hair colour; or why not blood type, or height? To open the dominant narrative to a wider array of contingencies, would challenge the privileged subject association that contemporary myths prescribe as knowledge based. As a result, anxieties formed due to an identity crisis would increase, creating a shift in the power relationships among the racial hierarchy within society.

It was only relatively recent that 'race' was restricted exclusively to physiognomy. As discussed previously in this thesis, 'race' was also interchangeable with religion, nation, class, and/or culture throughout various points in history. People within Europe were characterized along similar dimensions to groups of people outside of Europe

(Pieterse, 1995). Europeans had practiced racial languages that oppressed groups along shifting imaginary boundaries. Because of this, 'race' can be seen as interchangeable, contingent upon negotiated discursive assumptions. Indeed, classifying people along phenotypes or somatic differences, as a primary signifier, also carry the prescribed notions of secondary signified meanings within a dominant racial language.

SLIDING SIGNIFICATIONS AND THE LANGUAGE OF 'RACE'

Stuart Hall (1996) examines the power dynamic intrinsic to the ideological bias of 'race' as a socio-political construct. According to Hall (1996), 'race' has no taxonomic designation by virtue of a bio-genetic ascription. Despite this fact, 'race' survives as part of a contemporary Western vocabulary, loaded with harmful and oppressive ideological assumptions. These ideological assumptions about 'race' are manifest in discursive practices that have become validated through dominant Western myths.

The dominant myths, about 'race', contend that natural characteristics subsume value differences between groups along the lines of intelligence and behaviour. People who subscribe to these myths, living within the dominant culture, assume that 'race' is a real and viable form of classification that constitutes knowledge. According to this view it is perceived as commonsense that 'race' can be used as a form of obvious and natural distinction – both biologically and culturally. It is considered commonsense, therefore, that 'race' exists as a natural form of maintaining order among difference, within the existing social dynamic that serves to justify existing relations of power. This implies that a universal sense of permanence, attributed to these taxonomic divisions, is rooted in a racist colonialist discourse.

Stuart Hall (1996) claims that there is nothing static or absolute about 'race'. Constituted in language, its meanings are subject to the socio-political atmosphere of the historical environment that helps to create it. Because of this, meanings created about 'race' are always susceptible to change. Although classifications and categorizations are a fundamental human characteristic used to order meaning through language, these meanings are not absolute and should not be interpreted as such. Classifications and categorizations become especially problematic when they systematically attempt to justify existing power relationships as a way of maintaining an unjust social order by fixing differences. Once these differences are perceived as fixed, the corresponding systems of classification and categorization become taken-for-granted as myth. This is evident in the dominance of a social order based on the bio-genetic classification of 'race' as it has become and continues to be perpetuated through a dominant social myth. These myths can be revealed when the cultural artefacts in which they are coded are read as texts.

When read as a text, Hall (1996) perceives 'race' as working more like a language than a biological entity. As a result, 'race' can be seen as a discursive construct working as a sliding signifier (Hall, 1996). This statement can be best qualified through a brief examination of how meanings are produced through language and communication. During the production of meanings, through the discursive process of competition and negotiation of preferred readings, meanings can shift. This implies that 'race', as sliding signifier, cannot be fixed in its popular conception through bio-genetics. Grounded in language, meanings surrounding 'race' are continually susceptible to contested and negotiated perceptions that float through history. This means that the meanings surrounding the concept of 'race', as a 'floating signifier', are contextual and relative. Its meanings, therefore, are neither universal nor absolute. Race "floats within a sea of relational differences" (Hall, 1996). Given this premise, Hall (1996) has classified three main relational positions of difference for interpreting concepts about 'race'.

First, the Realist position believes that objective, bio-genetic differences exist, outside of language, and are accurately reflected in common sense systems of knowledge. This Realist position is commonly interpreted from within the culture that considers such claims as knowledge. Second, the Linguistic position, discounts any notions that objective, physical differences exist, within what people consider to be real outside of its construction in and through language. Within this second position, any differences that come into existence are a result of their construction in and through language. According to this position, language creates reality. A third position, however, considers that there are many material differences that exist in what we perceive as reality outside of language. It is only in and through systems of language that these differences become intelligible. Hall (1996) considers this third position to be discursive.

Subscribing to the Discursive position, Hall (1996) sees three major historical phases of discourse that attempted to – and still attempt to – justify power relations through the categories of racial hierarchy. All three phases try to fix differences as constitutive by absolute knowledge within the dominant myths of society. These differences are an attempt to make nature correspond with culture, by removing any historical context surrounding notions of 'race'. Indeed, these naturalized assumptions become part of a commonsense social discourse within each respective phase of understanding. For Hall (1996), these three epistemological phases are constitutive of the dominant discourses that have influenced and changed a given culture's perspective on the reality of 'race' over time.

As the first phase of knowledge, religion attempted to explain and fix perceived racial differences. When Europeans encountered people of the 'New World' there was a question of whether or not these 'new beings' were human like the Europeans. It became assumed and understood as commonsense that the indigenous populations of the 'New World' were of a different animal species created by God. Knowledge, in this case, was reflected and legitimated through religion. As Western empires realized that the new populations encountered could be somewhat assimilated into a Westernized culture by being converted to Christianity, religion no longer served to be an adequate explanation to fix cultural and somatic differences.

Anthropology served as the second phase of knowledge for understanding new populations of people. When it was determined that the people of the 'New World' were of the same species as the Europeans, it became assumed as common knowledge that these 'new people' were at a different stage of evolutionary development. The indigenous people of Africa and the Americas were believed to be closer to the original species, and were seen as 'missing links' on the evolutionary ladder that distinguished humans from primates. Anthropological assumptions, in this case, informed and determined commonsense, positioning Europeans at a higher stage of evolutionary development over 'people of colour'. When anthropology no longer provided a sufficient rationale to explain and fix the gulf of difference between the two populations, the collection of 'scientific' research and data was used in its place.

Science, as the third phase of knowledge, currently underlies much of our contemporary Western myths about 'race'. Subsuming previous religious and anthropological discourses about 'race', claims about modern science is often times used to justify and fix racial differences through the study of bone structure, blood factors and genetics.

V. THE SCIENCE OF OPPRESSION

COMPETING SCIENTIFIC PARADIGMS – A Contested Terrain of Inquiry

> *Scientific knowledge, like language, is intrinsically the common property of a group or else nothing at all. To understand it we shall need to know the special characteristics of the groups that create and use it.*
> (Kuhn, 1962, p. 210)

The theory and practice of Western Science, itself constructed within a discourse of related empiricisms (Kuhn, 1962), is subject to ideological scrutiny because it is born within a social and historical context and cannot be divorced from the environment of its conception (Adelman et.al, 2003). As the structure of science evolves, the bio-genetic reality of 'race' can even be challenged through contrasting scientific paradigms (Brace, 2000; Bamshad & Olsen, 2003). Because of this, the debate among biological anthropologists on the reality of 'race' is polarized.

Biological factors classifying people into distinct 'races' can yield many contradictory results. Forensic anthropologists, working with bone structure, believe that they can group people as originating from specific geographic regions. Based on this data, some of them believe that further inferences can be made on the type of 'race' that a person belongs to by matching bone structure with further speculations on other somatic features like skin colour (Gill, 2000). According to this belief, bone structure corresponds to commonly held assumptions about 'race' and is based on inheritable morphological attributes. For example, some forensic anthropologists believe that they can classify human skulls as belonging to distinct 'races'. Narrow nasal passages and eye sockets that are in close proximity to each other may indicate a Caucasoid, emphasized cheek bones may indicate a Mongoloid, and broad nasal passages "shaped like an upside down heart" may indicate that the skull belonged to a Negroid person (Rushton, 1995, 1996, 1998,

2000). On the other side of this debate, however, anthropologists studying blood factors disagree.

Serologists show that many biological traits cut across traditional racial boundaries. Phenotypical attributes such as skin, hair and bone, are distinct categories influenced by natural forces like climate. Blood-factor frequencies are not shaped by environmental forces in the same ways that skin, hair, and bone are. Serologists consider these physical variations among people as gradients of change known as clines (Brace, 2000). With physical variations in appearance being attributed to clines (as opposed to clearly distinguishable separations), it is impossible to conclusively delineate one group of people as distinct from another group of people. Differences in skin colour are gradual and seamless with no break in distinction from one geographical region to the next. Differences from 'white' skin to 'black' skin, rest on latitudinal orientation and exposure to the intensity of the sun's ultra violet rays. Without comparing extremes, it is hard to discern where one 'race' ends and another begins. Despite this fact, academics, intellectuals, and scientists alike, still ponder and debate imagined distinctions between populations by classifying them in terms of 'race' as a heritable, biological taxonomy. Many of these proponents have made a handsome career off such overtly racist and misleading notions. One of the leading proponents of 'race' – as a scientifically valid taxonomic concept – is Canada's own J. Philippe Rushton.

J. PHILIPPE RUSHTON AND THE EVOLUTIONARY PARADOX

John Philippe Rushton currently teaches as a tenured professor in the University of Western Ontario's Psychology department. Author of many controversial journal articles and books – like his most infamous *Race, Evolution and Behavior* – Rushton is one of Canada's hallmark figures in a hotly debated 'reality of race' argument. Rushton's (1995, 1996, 1998, and 2000) studies attempt to prove that by analysing proposed morphological and physiological differences between perceived 'races', scientists can accurately predict differences in intellectual potential and behavioural patterns – such as aggression and sexual restraint – that he believes can be attributed to differences between the respective racial categories. Furthermore, Rushton (1995, 1996, 1998, and 2000) believes that 'race' as a causal factor is not only scientifically verifiable within North America but is also consistent globally throughout time. This implies a universality and absoluteness to his findings that also highlights a glaring contradiction in his overall paradigm. This glaring contradiction – as I will return to shortly – ultimately leads his main arguments down a path of self destruction.

Rushton's (1995, 1996, 1998, and 2000) research, linking perceived racial differences to causal behavioural attributes and intelligence, places Asians at the more advanced end of the racial spectrum and Africans at the more primitive end. Europeans, in this framework, are curiously located consistently in between Asians and Africans. Furthermore, it is interesting to note that Europeans are not only located in the middle but are actually located in closer proximity to Asians than they are to Africans. His location of these three dominant racial categories is supposedly based on research that includes data from over 60 social and somatic variables. Some of these variables include: brain size gathered from the measurement and volume of skulls, the use of wet brain weight during autopsies, and scans from magnetic resonance imaging (MRI); intelligence based on IQ scores, and; sexual habits and temperament derived from the production of testosterone, just to list a few. Due to his own admission, the results interpreted from these variables, however, are not due to his own empirical studies but are derived instead from a compilation of studies done by other researchers – most of which are outdated and misconstrued. Nonetheless, these variables – among others according to Rushton – help him to 'scientifically' determine that intelligence and behavioural characteristics can be linked to existence of clearly delineable 'races'. Moreover, Rushton believes that his findings are conclusive based on the consistency and predictability of the results interpreted through his research framework. In order to reveal the contradictions intrinsic to his research, a closer look at how Rushton contextualizes 'race' should be examined.

Rushton's concept of 'race' is derived from the 18th century views of Swedish naturalist, Carolus Linaeus. Dividing the human species into four main categories – Asians, American Indians, Europeans, and Africans – variations on Linaeus' classification system is still commonly used in biology among many zoologists today. A definition of 'race' that is common to most zoologists implies that a variety or a subdivision exists in a given species. Variety that subdivides species is believed to occur naturally in a distinct combination of inherited physiological, biological, and morphological traits. When grouped together, such traits are interpreted as indicative of racial differentiation.

Although Linaeus' classification system identifies four main 'races' of the human species, some people would combine the categories that delineate Asians and American Indians into one 'race'. As a result, we are left with three main 'races' known respectively as Mongoloid, Caucasoid, and Negroid. These three 'races' form the basic categories through which Rushton operates within his research framework.

According to Rushton, racial differentiation occurs over long periods of time through evolution. As individuals within one group of people reproduce exclusively within their group, remaining confined to a specific geographical location, they are believed to have evolved distinct biological features – like skin colour – adapted as advantageous to the survival of the subspecies in their respective environment. As previously mentioned, these populations of subspecies are what zoologists consider to be 'races'. This conception of 'race', however, is commonly accepted as a misinterpretation of clinal variation between populations by many leading theorists in the scientific community (Adelman et.al, 2003; Brace, 2000; Bamshad & Olsen, 2003). What separate these scientists from Rushton are their views on how 'race' is interpreted.

For scientists like Rushton and Gill (2000), 'race' exists beyond simple arbitrary labels. 'Race', in this sense, is not only universal but it is also absolute. There is a contradiction inherent to the very thought of this statement within the accepted evolutionary paradigm of science. For instance, how can evolution – under its established principle of constant change, mutation or development based on environmental factors – be subject to stasis, as culminated in an absolute conclusion of a species' development?

To answer while clarifying this question, Rushton believes that three main 'races' exist as a result of the evolutionary development from a single population that originated in Africa. Rushton traces this development to outward migration that occurred as the original population reproduced and increased. According to this assumption, most people within the scientific community[13] commonly believe that Homo sapiens first appeared in Africa approximately 200,000 years ago. As this population reproduced and increased in size, they gradually migrated to Europe approximately 110,000 years ago and into Asia approximately 70,000 years later. Rushton (1995, 1996, 1998, and 2000) believes that the

---

[13] When I refer to 'the scientific community' I am by no means implying that consensus exists among all those claiming to be scientists. Rather, the 'scientific community' here loosely refers to a culture of professionals bound by empirical research methodologies that lead to postulations about consistency in observable phenomena. There is no singular 'scientific community' as there is no singular notion of culture. This term should not be taken outside of its generic construct.

evolutionary effects caused by these gradual migrations formed the three main racial groupings (Mongoloid, Caucasoid, and Negroid) that are conceptualized today.

Seeing that evolution indicates a continual state of development based on gradually shifting environmental factors, the perceived permanence about these three racialized categories is essentially arbitrary. Even though this process points to the arbitrary nature of classifying populations into distinct 'races', scientists like Rushton and others of his ilk use evolution to fix specious distinctions within human populations as objective and observable. Indeed, the use of evolution to qualify the existence of racial differences is tenuous at best and contradictory to say the least. The reason for this criticism is due to the fact that differences cannot be fixed if they *have* resulted from evolution simply because they must continue to be *subject* to evolution.

If differences within the human species – like those attributed to somatic distinctions commonly interpreted as 'race' – are evolutionary, there should be no objective and observable break from one population to the next. As a result, racial evolution occurs as a singular process within a species based on clines. Differentiation within a species, therefore, does not indicate the development of a subspecies but more so a clinal variation. Nonetheless, Rushton has made himself the authority on where the distinction between populations begins and ends by qualifying his arguments through an appeal to evolutionary principles in spite of this glaring contradiction. The contradictions inherent to using evolutionary theories, to explain the existence of distinct 'races', is further revealed in the ways that Rushton has trouble grouping the entire human population within his three narrow racial categories.

Although Rushton (1995, 1996, 1998, and 2000) believes that three main 'races' exist, he also acknowledges that these three main 'races' can be further subdivided in order to accommodate the logic of his belief in evolution. These further subdivisions are a result of increased spatial mobility across geographical boundaries and increased reproduction among populations in different geographical areas. Using this logic, the principles of evolution remains intact, in order to account for relatively recent mutations in populations that do not fall neatly into any of the three main categories. For example, Rushton (1998) has trouble classifying Hispanic or 'Latino' people.

As per Rushton's rigid classification system, Hispanics are neither European nor Asian. For Rushton (1998), they represent a further subdivision of the human species that indicates the admixture of a combination of racial attributes. According to Tim Wise from *Znet* (n.d.), however, 'Latino' is a term that refers to "an ethnic/ national/ regional/ heritage group within which skin color and racial phenotype varies dramatically". Anomalies of sorts, Hispanic and Latino people, for Rushton, are caught in a virtual limbo of evolutionary development, constituting the interstices of a flawed and arbitrary construct. By the logic of evolution, this further implies that the developments of new 'races' are constantly occurring phenomena. If this remains the case, how then can racial categories be anything but arbitrary?

Rushton's main 'races' – Mongoloid, Caucasoid, and Negroid – are perceived as universal and absolute. If this is the case, Rushton's research essentially contradicts the principles of evolution. Did evolution cease to work, as it has been for millions of years, as soon as J. Philippe Rushton appeared on the scene? Curiously, as Rushton claims to be a 'high priest' in the evolutionary science and genetics of 'race' – despite the fact that he has had no formal training in genetics – he surreptitiously manages to espouse a heretical logic against evolution all within the same research. Therein lies the contradiction inherent to Rushton's racial classification system that essentially undermines his very premise on 'race' as a causal factor.

Without solid evidence that distinct racial categories do in fact exist – as Rushton (1995, 1996, 1998, and 2000) has expertly conceptualized them – causal factors, like intelligence and behavioural attributes, that have been postulated as linked to these racial distinctions, quickly disintegrate from scientific knowledge claims and emerge as patent nonsense. If this is in fact nonsense masquerading as science, why do people like Rushton continue to make a living by misleading the public? The answer to this question is threefold and is based on: Rushton's convictions, sources of ample funding, and media hype.

In most cases researchers, conducting scholarly work or engaged in scientific inquiry, conduct their research under the belief that they are advancing knowledge in their respective field or discipline. As a result, researchers actually believe in the information that they have researched and therefore consider such findings to be knowledge. Clinging to the distortion that objective, observable phenomenon can be interpreted purely as it exists in reality, scientific researchers do not necessarily set out to intentionally mislead (Herman, n.d.). Indeed, Rushton has often tried to defend his research against implications that he is a racist, by claiming that he is simply a scientist that tries to reveal the truth. Perhaps his views are indicative of an underlying social psyche that yearns for some sort of validation towards hidden racist beliefs (Herman, n.d.). Maybe he doesn't realize that he is racist. Moreover, these hidden beliefs could possibly reveal a part of what Henry Giroux refers to as *White Panic* (Giroux, 1995). Either way, these views can be interpreted as bound in essence by what Herbert Marcuse (1969) refers to as the 'biology' of their discourse[14].

The 'biology' of a group's discourse is essentially how they make sense of the world around them in order to survive as it were. Knowledge in this sense, when interpreted under a more critical lens, is revealed as myth. The belief that 'race' is a biologically real entity becomes taken-for-granted as a natural fact. This occurs through the myth constructed about it and justified by the paradigm (Kuhn, 1962) that created it. Furthermore, propagating this myth about 'race' can also be profitable. This brings us to the second reason why some scientists make a living on flawed knowledge claims. There are underlying political and economic interests at stake, supporting the types of funding that keeps such research afloat.

Steve Buist (2000) exposes the fact that J. Philippe Rushton had received close to one million US dollars in funding during the 1990's from an organization called the Pioneer Fund. According to Buist (2000), the Pioneer Fund is an American organization that has a long legacy of funding 'race' research and eugenics. As mandated in its charter, the organization is dedicated to the notion of 'race betterment'. It becomes

---

[14] Herbert Marcuse (1969) criticizes capitalism in the ways that it has become rooted within the organic and instinctive nucleus of humanity. At this level, the mechanisms of global capitalism have been subsuming morality for profits. The dive for profits, in order to make a living, has become the basis to survival. This basis of survival has become entrenched at every dimension of social being, including the biological. Marcuse (1969) clarifies what he means by biological in his distinction of the term from a scientific discipline. For Marcuse (1969), biology and biological refers to a second nature of sorts. It represents the dimension of instinct and behaviour that become like vital needs to be satisfied in order for an organism to survive. Marcuse (1969) proposes the notion that Socialism must address the need towards revolution against global capitalism in order to be successful. Revolution must be enacted, not only in the social dimension but in the biological dimension also. However fitting for this section of the thesis, biology, in this sense, is not intended to be physiological. Although Marcuse's (1969) formulation of biology speaks to a Socialism that must counter global capitalism, I believe that his theories can be applicable to all forms of revolutionary struggle. In specific reference to this case, I have taken liberty to apply this notion of biology to a deep structured cultural instinct throughout Western science for fixing categories of 'race' as natural. Although there is no pun intended, the 'biology' of discourse is what I would like to refer to as myth, in the ways that it remains hidden in culture while organizing a perception of reality. To bring this analogy back to science, change can only occur when the myths propagated in one paradigm, encounter the myths propagated in another contesting paradigm (Kuhn, 1962).

abundantly clear that this notion of 'race betterment' implies the proliferation of white supremacist ideology through the sponsoring of scientific research that implies the existence of naturalized racial hierarchies. Even though Rushton currently holds a position on their executive board, he was not the only person funded. The Pioneer Fund sponsors other 'race' scientists, like Rushton, who demonstrate a penchant for research in the hopes that it can be used to prove a hierarchy among 'races'. Arthur Jenson, who has published research on why 'black' people have low IQ scores, happens to be another recipient of funding from this institute and pulls in even more financial support from the Pioneer Fund than Rushton (Buist, 2000).

With all the money to be made from wealthy and powerful racist organizations it is no surprise that 'race' myths are given voice that continues to be passed off as objective science. Whether or not these individuals who conduct this type of research are racist or politically motivated is not entirely the issue at hand. They will be the first to tell you that they are scientists and remain secluded in the world of science. They prefer to leave the policies and politics to politicians (Rushton, 1998, 2000). The curious thing about this statement is the fact that they have no problem accepting money from those who are politically motivated, who, in turn, intend to use the research that they fund to effect policy as in Herrnstein and Murray's (1994) *The Bell Curve*. Rushton's theories, coupled with the possibility that his research may be used to affect racist policies and incite tensions between racialized communities, have created a great deal of media hype in the popular press.

In a January 28th 1989 Toronto Star article titled "An obstinate professor and his theories on race. Race superiority theories pure hokum, scientists say", Rushton is quoted as saying:

> I'm not a policy maker and I'm not a racist. I just think government should be aware of differences between the races and take them into account when planning. The government may have to be more interventionist when dealing with these differences. (p. A8)

Although Rushton claims that he is not responsible for possible policies that his research may implicate, he is supportive of government using his findings to effect policy. Perhaps such policies could be aimed towards amending the existing policy of 'official multiculturalism' as it can be interpreted to be based on a familiar platform. Either way, Rushton's suggestion is problematic – not only in the implication that government policies should pander to the claims of racial superiority but more so based on the assumption that distinct 'races' do in fact exist.

On a deeper level, slightly removed from the overtly racist implications of Rushton's research, is the possibility and ease through which the government could potentially implement policy based on racial differences. After all – as previously discussed in this thesis – Canada's official policy on multiculturalism is a more subtle and purportedly more benign way of managing difference based on culture and/ or 'race'. Rushton's suggestion that government should consider basing policy on his 'race' research is promptly followed by scientists who claim that Rushton has misused their data, making any policy derived from such research problematic.

One aspect of Rushton's research – that *The Star* highlights as dubious based on the criticisms of scientists – is the premise that the more recently developed a 'race' is, the more advanced it is in many intellectual and behavioural respects. Seeing that Rushton posits all members of the human race as being evolved originally from Africa approximately 200, 000 years ago, he believes that Asians are the most recent to have evolved making them the most advanced sub-species of human. According to an article in *The Star,* scientists in the field of genetics and biochemistry consider the data used from this premise to be outdated and it has since been revised.

The revised data indicate that a second set of people from Africa have evolved last – even after Asians – making Rushton's evolutionary 'timing and advancement' theory null and void. The same article quotes University of California micro-biologist, Svante Paabo as saying, "I don't know if Dr. Rushton has accidentally or deliberately misunderstood our work on evolutionary dating. In any event this whole field is still highly speculative. To present it as scientific fact is wrong" (p. A8). Paabo goes on to say that "One thing we do know, however, is that it's ridiculous to compare races because they all emerged from one and there has been constant intermingling" (p. A8). This statement by Paabo is the only statement that *The Star* uses that derides Rushton's research on the belief that separate 'races' exist. Throughout the rest of *The Star's* coverage of Rushton, however, 'race' is assumed to be a natural fact where differences in 'race' are descriptive markers for different communities. If *The Star* were to place more emphasis on the illusion of 'race', Rushton's theories would quickly dissolve without all the added hype and spotlight. This is one clear example on how news is made and interpreted as opposed to being directly reported from objectively observed phenomena.

According to Richard Ericson, Patricia Baranek, and Janet Chan (1987), news is an interpretation of real phenomena that is structured through the organizational conventions that shape its discourse. As such, the facts presented in a news report are not self evident; the facts must be invested with significance (Ericson et al., 1987). Indeed, the creation of news involves a process of structuring reality. Although *The Star* article clearly makes the case that distinct 'races' do not exist because "they have all emerged from one", it nonetheless continues to use 'race' as descriptive categories that signify distinct communities. In this case, news is created in the insinuated beliefs that distinct communities of 'raced' individuals are subject to racism, without examining the ways in which racism structures racialized individuals into separate 'races'. Studies that question the scientific validity of 'race' can even be applied to Rushton's studies linking brain-size to intelligence.

With regards to Rushton's conclusions derived from brain size data, the same article mentioned above quotes University of Guelph neuro-psychologist Michael Peters as stating that there are "no reliable, racial brain-size studies" (p. A8). In my opinion *The Star* could emphasize this point in greater detail by stating a reason for this fact. The main reason that comes to mind as to why there are "no reliable, racial brain-size studies" could be that 'race' does not exist as an objective biological quality. Peters goes on to state that Rushton "compiles information without having any true expertise in the different specialties involved" (p. A8). Out of all the *Toronto Star* articles surveyed on the issue, this was the only article that discussed data that was used to challenge Rushton's research. This is rather telling with respect to the ways in which the public is informed about the issues surrounding Rushton's research and its broader social implications.

Instead of exposing the illusion of 'race' as a flawed premise within Rushton's research, *The Star* seemed content to promote an emotionally charged debate between Rushton and his critics. This angle was possibly deemed more newsworthy within the organizational structures that shape the discourse of news. As a result, this debate was presented as a 'hot ticket item' to be sold to large audiences. Headlines such as: "Teachers condemn Rushton's theory of racial inferiority"; "Rushton's credibility attacked by professors"; "An obstinate professor and his theories on race. Race superiority theories pure hokum, scientists say"; "Scholars dismiss Canadian's racial theory"; "Rushton's crime theories have no basis in fact", captured the spirit of the debate. By taking a closer look at these articles, however, most them – with the exception of two (one scarcely mentions that all people have evolved from one 'race' and the other, that happens to be an opinion letter to the editor, states that no pure 'races' exist) – insinuate the belief that distinct 'races' do in fact exist and Rushton's theories are racist under the premise that they attempt to justify a hierarchy among the 'races'. As a result, *The Star* managed to highlight the conflict and divisiveness between imagined racialized communities. Indeed, the Rushton coverage was quickly subsumed by questions of 'black' inferiority and 'white' superiority.

In a letter to the editor, published in the Opinion section of the March 14th 1989 issue, Julian Roberts and Thomas Gabor – from the University of Ottawa's Criminology department – represent a minority of people published in *The Star* that challenged the credibility of Rushton's theories on the premise that distinct 'races' exist in pure form. According to Roberts and Gabor, Rushton's theories of racial differences between 'blacks' and 'whites' are predicated on false assumptions about racial purity. Roberts and Gabor attempt to qualify this assertion by stating that "in North America, many blacks are more than half white by lineage and many whites have some black ancestry" (p. A21). This is a clear example of how racism is marketed primarily as a 'black'/ 'white' issue. Despite the fact that these scholars argue that there are no pure 'races', they do not attempt to discuss the presumed purity of Asians. This is crucial because, according to Rushton, Asians are on top of the evolutionary ladder of racial superiority. Although Roberts and Gabor do not go as far to say that 'races' do not exist, they do state that *pure* 'races' do not exist. Upon the basis of that assumption alone, Rushton's views are regarded as bogus science. Despite this criticism, however, commonly perceived racial groupings are still preserved in the ways that *The Star* continued to report on them.

In a March 15th 1989 article titled "Teachers condemn Rushton's theory of racial inferiority", Bob Mitchell of the *Toronto Star* writes that "most scientists insist there are no racial intelligence differences that are biologically determined, and that all racial genes come from the same evolutionary pool" (p. A7). Despite the admission that all "racial genes come from the same evolutionary pool", the article uncritically quotes Rosemary Clark – a secondary school teacher – as stating that "we have a significant amount of blacks and Orientals in our school ... I don't condemn research if it is academically done properly. But I do condemn any theory that ranks the races" (p. A7). This quote further supports the claim that 'races' are preserved as objective biological signifiers of identity. For Clark, the problem here is not that Rushton acknowledges the existence of distinct 'races' – the fact that "all racial genes come from the same evolutionary gene pool" is easily overshadowed by the assumption that different 'races' exist in nature. The problem for Clark is that Rushton's research pits the 'races' against each other according to a postulated evolutionary hierarchy.

In addition to the sensational debate that falls short of criticizing Rushton on the premise that distinct 'races' exist scientifically, *The Star's* coverage of the issues succeed in showcasing Rushton under a mass mediated spotlight. Moreover, the emotional tenor of the coverage sparked by this debate circuitously promotes Rushton's theories and elevates his personage to the rank of a sort of infamous celebrity. As a now famous scholar, Rushton's work reaches a wider, more popular audience beyond the walls of academia. Indeed, albeit largely negative, Rushton is given a greater voice through which to express his ideas.

On February 17th 1989, *The Star* published an article on the front page titled "Rushton called a racist at Geraldo taping". Dan Smith of the *Toronto Star* reports that "Canada's most controversial academic steadfastly denied heated charges that he was a racist" (p. A1). According to Smith, the Geraldo show titled "Sex, Brains and Brawn: Is there a Master Race?" was scheduled to air on March 8th 1989 on "more than 190 North American TV stations, by far the biggest vehicle the formerly obscure Rushton has gained to publicize his controversial views" (p. A2). Smith reports that the taping of the show was denounced as "a circus or worse" by "every major participant but the producers" (p. A1). Ironically enough, however, although Smith's tone appears to be critical of the media "circus" surrounding Rushton on the Geraldo show, as a venue to further propagate his racist views, he nonetheless adds to Rushton's publicity by alerting *The Star's* readership, in advance, to the exact time and date that the show was aired.

By further contributing to Rushton's publicity, dominant points of his research are highlighted in most of the articles concerning him. Few articles, however, take the time to systematically deride his work on the level of sound scholarship. In a March 19th 1989 editorial titled "A weak reaction to academic fraud", *The Star* is quite caustic in its displeasure over Rushton's right to academic freedom without detailing expert data that proves his work fraudulent. According to *The Star* it is "without exception" that the "academic community" has found Rushton's conclusions to have no "scientific basis" (p. A28). Although it is widely publicized that Rushton's research is not based in science, as it purports to be, there is no mention in this article that his research is based on secondary sources that have been largely misconstrued. As a result, *The Star* has labelled Rushton a "charlatan" and the UWO senate decision "preposterous" in their dereliction of their broader duty to protect society (p. A28). To further emphasize the perceived threat that

Rushton poses to society, *The Star* employs sensational tactics to appeal to the emotions of its readership.

Despite Rushton's strong convictions towards his research findings, the financial support he received to conduct his research, and the subsequent media hype that inadvertently promoted his work, it is important to note, however, that not all science surrounding notions of 'race' is one sided. Despite *The Star's* limited coverage of sound scholarly criticisms, some of the very evidence espoused by Rushton that he considers conclusive, is subject to contested interpretations even within the very scientific community that he claims membership to.

GENETICS OF 'RACE' – Science Fact or Fiction?

When using somatic factors like skin colour to group people into 'races', Europeans can be interpreted as having more in common, biologically, with Chinese than either of them have in common with Africans. If the distributions of blood-factors are used, Africans and Europeans have more in common with each other biologically than either of them does with Chinese. Although similarities in physiological features within regions can be used towards positing ancestry, current genetic research reveals that 90% of human genetic variation occurs within a population whereas there is only 10% variation between populations (Bamshad & Olsen, 2003).

University of Utah physician Michael Bamshad and science writer Steve Olsen (2004), use genetics to illustrate how common notions of 'race' are actually clinal. Bamshad and Olsen (2004) subscribe to the popular 'out of Africa' theory which states that over the past hundred thousand years, people had migrated all over the world from Africa. The regions where people have settled, has created distinct genetic signatures in deoxyribo nucleic acid (DNA) based on environmental conditions. Their research further reveals that variations in the base pairs that form the building blocs of DNA – polymorphisms – are common and do not directly affect physical traits.

Scientists who have sequenced the human genome (full set of DNA) have identified millions of different polymorphisms. Although distribution of these polymorphisms across populations, reflect the history of a population and the environmental effects of natural selection on them, 68% of all genes are identical between humans, exhibiting no polymorphic variation (Wise, n.d.). To use this data to group 'races' of people would imply that certain polymorphisms would be present in all members of a group, while absent in all members of other groups (Bamshad & Olsen, 2004).

According to Tim Wise of *Znet* (n.d), people who are perceived to be on opposite ends of the 'race' spectrum – 'blacks' and 'whites' – share 96.8% of the genetic code with a maximum of 0.032 variations in genes between the perceived groupings. Differences between perceived groups, on the basis of genetic makeup, are far too miniscule to indicate distinct speciation among human populations. Bamshad and Olsen (2004) believe that groups have separated too recently, and mixed too much, for differences based on natural selection to have any significance. Moreover, this research shows that outward physical appearances are largely insignificant regarding a person's genetic makeup.

Although physical features such as skin colour and hair texture, combined with geographical origin and culture, are commonly used to group people into racial categories, common traits, such as skin and hair, can be regarded as "family resemblance writ large" (Brace, 2000). Further more, these 'family resemblances' vary gradually between populations. Supporting this claim, population genetics provides evidence that less than 1% of genes can be linked to heritable somatic features like skin colour (Wise, n.d.). Given this assertion, there are no bio-genetic racial differences; there are only clines which make racial distinctions between neighbouring populations virtually imperceptible. As a result of widespread scientific consensus on the uselessness of commonly perceived racial categories, the use of physical features like skin colour and hair texture to organize human populations are purely trivial. Despite this data, a minority of scientists like Rushton continue to cling to these distortions of racial difference to make sweeping generalizations on intelligence and the predictability of behavioural traits based on genes.

According to Bamshad and Olsen (2004), however, it is not only misleading to assume that categorizing the human species into groups based on these traits is somehow linked to the genes that a person is born with; it is even more misleading to use these data to determine intelligence or predict social behaviours. Genes cannot be used to group people into racial categories. Furthermore, using genetic data one cannot interpret such categories as universal or absolute. 'Race' is more so a product of language than it is a product of science (Hall, 1996). This is seen in the ways in which different populations interpret and label racial difference.

The definition of what constitutes membership in racial categories varies from region to region. The same person who may be considered 'black' in the United States, may be seen as 'white' in Brazil or 'coloured' in South Africa – where 'coloured' is a term used to categorize a group that is distinguishable from both 'black' and 'white' (Bamshad & Olsen, 2003; Daniels, 1996). How groups are distinguished in difference to one another depends on what genes are isolated and examined. A person may be categorized into one group based on skin colour and at the same time considered part of another group based on hair texture. This implies that there is greater genetic variance *within* culturally perceived racial groups than there are *between* them. Although people may appear similar on the surface, within the commonly perceived racial group, they can be quite different genetically.

The people living in sub-Saharan Africa and the Aboriginal people of Australia share a similar skin complexion but are very dissimilar genetically. Likewise, two groups that share a similar genetic makeup may be exposed to different environmental factors that exaggerate their differences. Furthering this claim, in a study that isolated polymorphisms used to estimate the percentage of genes originating from a continental region, it was discovered that on average, Americans who considered themselves 'white' had less than 90% European ancestry according to genetics (Bamshad & Olsen, 2003). This implies that common perceptions of 'race' are not absolutely reflective of a person's genetic heritage. For Bamshad and Olsen (2003), the value and importance of perceived racial differences are shaped by social and political impressions and not scientific ones. Despite these findings – amidst all the media hype propagated about racist scientists and their research – the *Toronto Star* has not only been slow to report on these issues but articles that question the reality of 'race' have been scarce.

An article published on October 13th 1996 titled "Scientists find we are all the same under the skin: No genetic basis for race, say researchers", offers rare coverage on the genetic argument that proves all people evolved from the same 'race'. According to Robert Boyd, in a special article to *The Star*, "most scientists now reject the concept of race as a valid way to put human beings into separate groups" (p. A14). Despite widespread public opinion on the issue, this general scientific consensus comes about through "spectacular advances in molecular biology and genetics" and is a culmination of work that has been gathered since the 1970's (p. A14). Quoting Yale geneticist Kenneth Kidd, "DNA data supports the concept that you can't draw boundaries around races" (p. A14). Contrary to widespread scientific belief, however, the article does mention that a small number of researchers – including Philippe Rushton – still cling to the flawed genetic concept of 'races'. It is ironic that this article points out that Rushton still clings to a distorted view that distinct 'races' exist, despite the fact that *The Star* reproduces the same racialized distinctions in other stories.

Another rare *Toronto Star* article that reports on how current genetic studies have disproved the bio-genetic concept of 'race' was published on June 30th 2000. This article, titled "The other genome project: search for human diversity proves we're similar after all", was published in the midst of the media's coverage of the Human Genome Project. Although the Human Genome Project mainly focused on mapping the entire DNA code for the purpose of medical advancement, the Human Diversity Genome Project[15] applied much of this information to explore the nuances of human differences between populations. According to Delthia Ricks and Bryn Nelson, in their special to *The Star*, "the project has found no biological basis for the concept of race. Physical differences such as skin colour and hair texture are adaptations to the environment spelled out in infinitesimal variations of the same code we all share" (p. F2). This article, however, makes no direct mention of the White House press conference on June 26th 2000, where J. Craig Venter – president and chief scientific officer of Celera Genomics (the private

---

15 For more information on the Human Diversity Genome Project, please visit the website at Hhttp://www.stanford.edu/group/morrinst/hgdp/faq.htmlH.

company that headed the government's Human Genome Project) – announced that his team of scientist have sequenced the entire human genome.

At the press conference, Venter (2000) announced that his team of scientists had sequenced the genetic code of three females and two males. This sample of people identified themselves as Hispanic, Asian, Caucasian, or African-American. According to Venter (2000), "We did this sampling not in an exclusionary way, but out of respect for the diversity that is America, and to help illustrate that the concept of race has no genetic or scientific basis"[16]. Of the five genomes sequenced, the data remains conclusive that there is no way to determine 'race' or ethnicity as genetically distinct from one another. On the level of genetics, individuals are all unique due to minute variations in each genome. Population statistics, therefore, do not apply.

The fact that some of these arguments only managed to garner scarce coverage as opposed to several articles questioning the social implications of its research – as seen in *The Star's* earlier coverage of Rushton – illustrates a rather telling example of the mainstream media's success in marginalizing the issue. This can be further insinuated in *The Star's* uncritical, yet continued use of racial categories in their expose` of racial profiling to be discussed in a later chapter of this thesis.

The Star's continued use of racial categories in their coverage exhibits a sort of institutional amnesia. Either it does not remember that 'race' is a social construct or it refuses to remember in order to create a more sensational story. As discussed earlier in this chapter, the news is not a reflection of reality but an interpretation of it (Ericson et al.,

---

[16] For the full White House press conference, please refer to the Human Genome Project Information website provided through the White House Office of the Press Secretary at
<Hhttp://www.ornl.gov/sci/techresources/Human_Genome/project/clinton2.shtmlH>
This website is sponsored by the U.S. Department of Energy Office of Science, Office of Biological and Environmental Research, and the Human Genome Program.

1987). *The Star* continues to use 'race' as an analytic and discursive concept – commonly interpreted as normal via consensus – as being rooted in an objective reality. Despite its publication of the two articles on the genetic studies that disprove 'race', in subsequent accounts of 'race' *The Star* continues to reinforce a commonly distorted view that does not essentially challenge the status quo.

Without challenging popular notions of 'race' and re-educating the public in the process, *The Star* misses its opportunity to reveal new truths that may have a profound social impact in the struggle against racism. Even though it barely recognizes the fact that other truths about 'race' currently exist in the form of popular scientific knowledge, these truths are marginalized and quickly forgotten. Indeed, 'races' and assumptions surrounding 'race' are essentially ideological, discursive constructs. Despite beliefs now popular among most scientists, distorted notions of 'race' persist and have become deeply enmeshed within the discourses of our dominant myths that shape our perceptions of reality and ourselves through language.

VI. LIVING THROUGH LANGUAGE

REALITY & 'RACE' – Making Sense of Our Existence through Language

> *To speak...means to above all assume a culture,*
> *to support the weight of a civilization*
> (Fanon, 1967, pp. 17-18)

The notion of myth has many implications regarding the ways that we interpret our experiences as subjects within the world. That being said, myth is intimately tied to notions of knowledge and reality. Using terms like *see* and *interpret*, knowledge, myth, and reality are revealed by the ways that meanings are constructed through language. This is explored in the common discourses of 'race' as historical constructs of Western imperialist ideologies.

Like social constructivist notions of reality, 'race' exists as a fluid concept constituted in a discourse of ideas. This means that there is no physiological, bio-genetic merit to its concept. It exists as an abstraction, through systems of language and representation that constitute ways of ordering and interpreting the world through myth. Given this assertion, 'race' is as *real* as the theories that bind it within the confines of its respective social framework. This theory has very salient implications for the ways that 'race' is represented in the mass media.

The following part of this thesis continues from where my analysis left off in the previous chapter. There, I outlined the ways that the *Toronto Star* reported on issues of 'race' through the hype generated about Philippe Rushton and its subsequent yet scarce coverage of genetics and 'race'. The information presented in this part of the thesis attempts to further explore the ways that myths construct a *reality* of 'race' in the popular press through a critical discourse analysis of selected Toronto Star articles from its coverage of racial profiling. Here, I intend to further reveal myth by demystifying the common meanings associated in the ways in which *The Star's* codes a language about 'race'. Before proceeding with an analysis of the ways myth works to construct and perpetuate distorted notions of 'race', it is important that a clear understanding of the terminology surrounding this study be elucidated.

LANGUAGE & DISCOURSE – A Brief Description

Language broadly refers to entire systems of signs as "a principle of classification" (Saussure, 1996a, p. 39). The science of linguistics, rooted in semiotics, studies the structural anatomy of signs and sign systems including words (spoken and written), symbols, and images (Cohan & Shires, 1996). Incorporating the use of language and the practice of how meanings are circulated through interpretive communities of ideas, leads to discourse.

Discourse refers to the use of language within a formalized, ideological framework (Cohan & Shires, 1996). Articulated through the use of language, it indicates a form of cohesion in the relationship between signs and their meanings. Through this cohesion, discourse contextualizes the ideas formed about an object or concept, as steeped in relations of power. For Paul Bove (1995), discourse in criticism is "the organized and regulated, as well as the regulating and constituting, functions of language that it studies: its aim is to describe the surface linkages between power, knowledge, institutions, intellectuals, the control of populations, and the modern state as these intersect in the functions of systems of thought" (pp. 54-55). In this sense, discourse is an active vessel of ideology.

CONCEPTUALIZING IDEOLOGY – From Ideas to Practice to Resistance

Although there are different definitions of **Ideology** used to accomplish different theoretical ends, it broadly refers to a system of beliefs derived from the process of producing meanings and ideas. These systems of beliefs can be attributed to specific classes or groups. Socially determined, ideologies carry the weight of cultural values and attitudes (Fiske, 1990). To understand the depth and scope of ideology, it is useful to articulate some of the concepts that have evolved through its rich history.

Arising for the first time out of the French Revolution, the term *ideology* is the English translation for the French term *ideologie*. The term was coined by the French rationalist philosopher Antione Destutt de Tracy to imply a 'science of ideas' (Kavanagh, 1985). Since its first use during the French revolution, the term has evolved in its complexity, beyond references to mere 'ideas', encompassing the driving force behind real material and historical conditions of existence. This notion of ideology had since gained popularity in Marxist theories (Fiske, 1990).

According to John Fiske (1990), Karl Marx used the term ideology to imply a set of ideas that lead to a false consciousness. This notion of a false consciousness attempted to explain the ways in which the ideas of the ruling class were imposed on the working classes. This notion of a false consciousness, however, is commonly misinterpreted in its oversimplification and erroneously ascribed to the writings of Marx.

According to Terry Eagleton (1991), Marx never actually used the phrase 'false consciousness.' The phrase was used by his colleague Frederick Engels in a letter to Franz Mehring in 1893 (Eagleton, 1991). Engels viewed ideology as a process of false consciousness, implying that the true motives driving the social agent was masked behind sets of surface motives. For Eagleton (1991), ideology in this regard is a form of "rationalization – a kind of double motivation, in which the surface meaning serves to block from consciousness the subject's true purpose" (p. 89). In this context, ideology is socially determined thought that essentially denies its determinacy.

Seeing that ideology is socially determined thought that denies its determinacy, the veridical quality of consciousness is layered in purity to the degree from which it is based in the historical and material conditions of existence. As a result, the 'real' or 'true' motives that impel social actors are a form of consciousness derived from 'real' historical and material circumstances. Denying the social determinacy that such thoughts carry, by distancing consciousness from the historical and material circumstances of existence, ideology can be interpreted as a form of self deception that masks the historical and material conditions of a class-based society. Ideology, in this regard, can be interpreted as political rather than epistemological. The importance of ideology, therefore, lies in the function and origin of such thoughts and not necessarily in the veracity of its character per se. Indeed, the "falsity of ideology in this context, is the falsity of class rule itself" (Eagleton, 1991, p. 90).

For Marx (1970), "the ideas of the ruling class are in every epoch the ruling ideas" (p.128). Indeed, Marx (1970) considered ideology to be a tool used by the ruling class, to manage the working class population within a system that oppresses them. Being intimately connected to the economic means of production, Marx (1970) believed that the rational science of historical materialism would eventually counter the ideology of the ruling class, leading the working classes to realize their material conditions of oppression by virtue of a class consciousness. Once the working classes could develop a class consciousness – realizing the root and function of their oppression – Marx (1970) assumed that they would inevitably revolt against the very system of oppression imposed upon them by the ruling class. As soon as this working class revolt against ruling class oppression was to become successful, Marx (1970) envisioned that the working classes would eventually usher in a new epoch of a classless society that would no longer need the ruling class ideology. As history progressed further into the 20th century, however, it became evident that Capitalism would not be overthrown by a rational realization of the economic forces of oppression. To accommodate for this anomaly, a second generation Marxist, Louis Althusser, developed a more refined concept of ideology.

According to Althusser ideology was not simply a set of ideas but a ubiquitous, ongoing practice in which all social classes were active participants (Fiske, 1990). To clarify Althusser's position, the ruling class participated in the production and dissemination of ideology while maintaining their social status of privilege over the working class. The working class, likewise, also participated in the production and dissemination of ideology, contributing to their position of subordination and oppression. As strange as it might have seemed that subordinated classes participated in their own oppression, ideology, nonetheless, was understood as working implicitly from within the deeply inscribed ways of thinking and living. As a result, ideology was believed to be internalized by all classes (Turner, 1992) and it could no longer be considered the exclusive tool that the ruling class used to explicitly subjugate the working class. The process by which the working class contributed to their subordination was achieved through what Althusser called **interpellation** (Fiske, 1990).

For Althusser, interpellation was the practice of calling or hailing readers of a message to take a position within the ideological framework of a respective social relation (Fiske, 1990). Through interpellation, social relations of power, dominance and subjugation, were automatically maintained. Because of interpellation, subjects or readers would sometimes take the position of an ideological category other than their social one. This implied that the dominant ideology was working at its best especially when it was accepted by all social classes while maintaining existing relations of power by consent. In this model of inexorable ideological frameworks, resistance was seen as futile and successful campaigns of resistance were considered improbable due to a lack of agency on the part of the interpolated subject. To account for the possibility of successful campaigns of resistance, the work of another second-generation Marxist, Antonio Gramsci, deserves attention.

According Gramsci (1992), ideology was considered a terrain of constant struggle and was characterized by a concept known as hegemony (Fiske, 1990; Turner, 1992). Placing emphasis on "resistance and instability", **hegemony** involved a constant dialectic of "winning and re-winning" of majority consent (Fiske, 1990) to the systems that oppress them. The ideologies of the dominant class (a social minority) were seen as constantly working to win the consent of the subjugated classes (a social majority). As a result, continual resistance was created in the social relations of class experience.

The experiences of the subordinated classes – characterized by a combination of race, gender, sexual orientation, etc. – would oftentimes contradict the material and historical experiences that the dominant class imposed on them through an ideology about them. These dominant ideologies about everyday social relations constituted what was known as commonsense (Fiske, 1990). In short, although the real material conditions, experienced by the subjugated, were not necessarily consistent with what the dominant class told them their experiences should be, hegemony created a model of ideology where commonsense prevailed through the constant struggle for consent. This created gaps in the apparently seamless production and dissemination of ideology. These gaps allowed the perfect opportunities for conflict, struggle and resistance. Ideology was therefore marked by volatile social relations.

In Gramsci's (1992) model, although resistance has created the possibility to overcome various struggles, such struggles could never completely be eliminated. Considering a hybrid definition of all three of these models of ideology, it is safe to explore the ways that ideologies work through Roland Barthes' notion of myth as a class based structure that naturalizes existing social relationships.

THE SEMIOTICS OF MYTH – Meaning & the Process of Signification

Myth refers to 'a chain of related concepts' (Fiske, 1990), appropriated by a culture or group, that provides a framework for interpreting experience. According to Roland Barthes (1972, 1984), ideology is the source of second-order meanings manifested through myth. As a result, myth is seen as a central part of cultural perspective that is unquestionable. Taken-for-granted as reality, myth informs a world view. Following a tradition of semiologists like Ferdinand de Saussure (1996), Barthes (1968, 1972, and 1984) extends the field of semiotics, conceptualizing myth as a second-order among two orders of signification.

The first-order of **signification** refers to the systematic relationships created between the sign and the mental perception or image of the object that it is understood to represent in an external reality (Barthes, 1968). The sign is split into two parts, the signifier and the signified. The **signifier** is the physical representation of the sign itself constituting its form (Barthes, 1968). 'TREE', in its physical written form, is a combination of marks forming letters on a page. These marks on the page can be taken further to represent letters forming a word. If taken for more than just marks on the page, the word 'TREE' becomes signified in a mental concept that alludes to *tree-like* qualities. **Signified** represents the content of a sign through the mental concept formed about the word 'TREE' (Barthes, 1968). The process of first-order signification is the theoretical correlation of the physical sign ('TREE'- signifier) to the mental image (signified) that is understood to refer to an object in reality (mental image of a wooded plant that exists in an external reality – exuding tree-like qualities signified). At an elementary level, the process of first-order signification is one way of organizing reality. The term that Barthes (1996) used to refer to Saussure's (1996) notion of first-order signification is denotation.

Denotation, as a first-order of signification, becomes the most obvious, commonsense meaning attributed to a sign (Barthes, 1996). The word 'TREE' denotes a mental image that is understood as referring to a physical object in an external reality that exudes tree-like qualities. Regardless of the possible ways that a specific word is written (TREE, *TREE, tree,* tree), it denotes the same object. This order of signification, however, does not address the ways that signs can be interpreted beyond their relation to other signs. It does not take into account how signs are used to create meanings within culture.

Although Barthes (1972, 1984, and 1996) was not only concerned with signs and their relation to other signs, he was primarily concerned with the relationships that these signs had once inserted into culture. In order to address this concern, Barthes (1968, 1996) extended Saussure's (1996a) process of signification to a second level. In the second-order of signification, Barthes (1972, 1984, and 1996) studied the ways that signs worked in two ways: myth and connotation.

Connotation occurs when a sign is absorbed into the value system of a culture (Barthes, 1996). Because of this, meanings become more than objective reflections of an external reality. They become inter-subjective. The sign alone does not affect the reader. Readers are affected as much by the sign itself, as they are in the ways that the sign is presented to them. For example, a picture of a tree may focus on its foliage bearing fruit. This image may connote food. Another photograph of the same tree may frame it in such a manner that it casts a long shadow over the ground. This image may connote refuge. Denotation addresses *what* a sign represents, whereas connotation addresses *how* a sign is represented (Fiske, 1990). Connotation is the second-order meaning of the signifier, whereas myth is the second-order meaning of the signified.

In contemporary Western vocabulary, myth has come to be conceptualized in reference to false stories or fables. Contrary to this notion, Barthes (1972, 1984) used the term myth to imply "a story by which a culture explains or understands some aspect of reality or nature [...] a chain of related concepts" (Fiske, 1990, p. 88). According to Barthes (1972, 1984), the concept of myth has many implications about the perceptions of knowledge and reality within society:

> Semiology has taught us that myth has the task of giving an historical, intention a natural justification, and making contingency appear eternal. What the world supplies to myth is a historical reality, defined ... by the way in which men [sic] have produced or used it; and what myth gives in return is a natural image of reality ... A conjuring trick has taken place; it has turned reality inside out, it has emptied it of its history and has filled it with nature, it has removed from things their human meaning so as to make them signify human insignificance (Barthes, 1972, pp. 142-143).

One of the most salient features of myth is the ways in which it takes hold of an object or subject and works to naturalize it, distancing it from a culture or history about it. According the second-order of signification, the reality of objects is articulated in and through language; and language is ideologically entrenched in the social classes of tradition. While, history becomes socio-politically distinguished from nature, myths serve to naturalize a language about objects, disguising their socio-political roots as a-historical. As a result, Barthes (1984) considers myth to be de-politicized speech.

As a form of depoliticized speech, myth masks the objects they refer to under the guise of natural semblance. This obscures any cultural link that an object may have to the material and historical conditions of its class-based, interpretive dimension. Because of its natural semblance, myth makes the objects it colonizes appear eternal and absolute. According to Edward Said (1978), "myth does not analyse or solve problems…It presents them as already analysed and solved; that is, it presents them as already assembled images…"(p. 312). As uniform as these qualities appear to present myth, it would be a mistake, however, to assume that all forms of myth are the same. Towards the end of *Mythologies,* Barthes (1972) conceptualized differences between 'myth on the right' and 'myth on the left'. Before unpacking what is meant by 'myth on the left' versus 'myth on the right', it is important to preface their meanings as forms of speech that reveal what myth *is* in relation to what myth *is not.*

If we recall, Barthes (1972) considers myth to be depoliticized speech. An inversion of this definition would posit political speech as the direct opposite of myth. To clarify what is meant by political language is to articulate forms of speech that attempts to transform nature/ reality. By this I mean that political language is transitive in its relation to nature/ reality. Contrary to this notion, however, de-politicized language is a second-order language that articulates the actions of the first. Indeed, it exhibits an intransitive relationship to nature/ reality. Although this second-order language is not entirely mythic, it does form the environment where myth can colonize objects already mediated through the first-order of signification. In this respect, a language that is not mythical can be seen in the acts of revolutionary speech as highly politicized and transitive. They are transitive in so much as they try to affect change in nature/ reality as opposed to preserving an image of nature/ reality. Indeed, not all forms of language are mythic however.

According to Barthes (1972), revolutionary language cannot be mythic in the sense that revolutionary acts are intended to reveal the material and historical dimensions of nature/ reality through politicized articulations as opposed to naturalized presuppositions. Indeed, it does not attempt to mask the political aspects of objects as natural, producing myth; rather it attempts to reveal the political aspects of objects, demystifying myth. Now that myth is determined in relation to what it is not, different forms of myth can be discussed by distinguishing 'myth on the right' from 'myth on the left'.

For Barthes (1972), 'myth on the left' – once characterized by revolutionary speech – attempts to distort and mask its revolutionary qualities. As a result, it settles, ex-nominated, as an alternative form of naturalized, de-politicized speech. 'Myth on the left', however, is not essential in its propagation throughout the vast scope of everyday social relations. As a matter of convenience, it invests its focus in the rarities of political life. As a result, it is ephemeral and limited in scope. This is due in large respects to its association with the oppressed classes, whose primary language is that of a revolutionary quality. In this respect, 'myth on the left' is obvious and not as discrete as 'myth on the right'.

'Myth on the right' is characterized by de-politicized speech from the first moment it takes hold of objects in culture. There are no forms of revolutionary speech that preface its existence. As such, 'myth on the right' essentially proliferates itself ceaselessly, remaining ex-nominated in its process of colonizing the nuances of everyday social relations. Indeed, language used by 'myth on the right' does not intend to transform; rather it aims at masking the social, historical, and political dimensions of objects by eternalizing them as natural.

Although there are no significant inner differences between the respective myths, there are varying degrees of proliferation within them. As a result, some myths expand better than others depending on their respective social atmosphere. For instance, apartheid – in its institutionalized form of segregated differences – is a system where a master 'race' would exclusively reap the benefits of social, political and economic privilege. In this respect, the myths central to apartheid could only proliferate within the confines of an overtly racist society. In comparison, multiculturalism – in its institutionalized form of segregated differences – is a theory where the notion that different cultures/ 'races' are believed to equally exist in privileged competition for social, political, and economic benefits. In this respect, the myths central to multiculturalism could proliferate widely throughout all societies that subscribe to a 'liberal' ideology. Both of these scenarios are bound by myths about 'race'. They vary slightly, however, in the ways in which such myths are interpreted and used within their respective social context. Either way, myth offers a useful subject to critically explore cultural narratives through a detailed textual analysis.

A textual analysis that reveals myth in cultural narratives, attempts to demystify the stories cultures use to understand their reality. As discussed above, there are varying levels of effectiveness in the proliferation of myth. As seen in the example using the proliferation of racial myths in multiculturalism, myths used in 'liberal' societies are often very discrete. In order to demystify discrete myths, as seen in more 'liberal' settings, Barthes (1972, 1984) offers some useful rhetorical forms to analyze through which mythic signifiers can be arranged. An example of a rhetorical form can be seen through Barthes' (1984) notion of inoculation.

Through inoculation, myth incorporates an incidental flaw within a class-based society in order to better conceal a principle flaw. For example, the racist practices of 'a few bad apples' are sacrificed in the interests of preserving the racisms lived within the greater 'liberal' society. As discussed in an earlier chapter of this thesis, the beating death of a Somali youth by a Canadian soldier was punishable as an individual act of racism. Even though the Canadian soldier who murdered the Somali youth was considered by most people to be a member of an oppressed class, subsequent inquiries about the individual act did not raise questions as to the 'impressive ideological formations' that enabled the act to occur within a broader structure of imperial racisms. The individual act, as a signifier of the broader lifestyle was removed from the larger historical context of colonization. This brings us to a second rhetorical form of myth.

Myth positions the object or subject that it speaks of as separate from history. In the example using the beating death of the Somali youth, any sense of a colonial memory evaporates during a formal inquiry into the events leading up to the tragedy. It is as though the events transpired in a vacuum, robbing a Western institution of any sense of collective responsibility. As a result, myth appears as a statement of fact, leading us to a third rhetorical form.

As a statement of fact, myth appears without any further explanation. The Canadian soldier who beat the Somali youth to death was not just practising an act of racism – racism being a practice external to who he is, already fully defined. The Canadian soldier practiced an act of racism because he is a racist. Not only is racism a part of who he is, it is also a part of the collective history he shares with other members of armed services who have been socialized within a racist society. Racism, in this case, does not offer a self-contained definition. There is more to racism than the individual act. In this scenario, notions about racism had been colonized by myth.

Myth colonizes an object or subject within culture as a fully formed sign that requires no further definition beyond the way it is presented. As a result, myth becomes invisible, working beyond the conscious perceptions of the groups that employ them within their given context. Latent beneath the historical layers of its conception, myths mask the roots of its social construction by appealing to convention.

> Myth does not deny things, on the contrary, its function is to talk about them, makes them innocent, it gives them a natural and eternal justification, it gives them a clarity which is not that of an explanation but that of a statement of fact … it organizes a world without contradictions because it is without depth, a world wide open to and wallowing in the evident, it establishes a blissful clarity: things appear to mean something by themselves (Barthes, 1972, pp. 142-143).

Considering myth in a textual analysis of cultural narratives, the analyst is primarily concerned with unveiling the historical dimensions of reality. In order to achieve this task, the analyst must expose and articulate the relationships between language's content, and the ways that meanings are constructed around the cultural assumptions imbedded in language's form. In so doing, the analyst must be aware that language carries ideological assumptions that appear to be natural; void of historical context. This type of analysis reveals the gaps intrinsic to class struggle that ideology attempts to mask through myth itself. Given this fact, myth necessarily shifts as soon as it enters a stream of consciousness as myth. The existence of myth relies on a conception of knowledge and reality that necessitates its latency. In order to exist as such, myths must essentially be undetected.

In order to become aware of myth, the analyst must shift focus from the content of the story, to the relationship between the form and content of the story. Analyzing myth in cultural narratives requires a shift in perspective from the natural to the socially constructed. As a result, the analyst must focus on the rhetorical forms in which mythic signifiers become situated through a meta-language.

DISCOURSE, A MYTHIC META-LANGUAGE

According to Barthes (1968, 1972, 1984, and 1996), mythic language is a meta-language. In this regard, a meta-language is a second-order language used to articulate the first (Gaines, 2001). Analyzing meta-language can reveal the historical and ideological context that meanings are constructed in. Seeing that meanings are imbedded within cultural texts and become naturalized through convention, the focus on meta-language in textual analysis, allows the analyst to interpret the everyday aspects of cultural life in new ways. Through a critical perspective, the obvious, mundane aspects of everyday life are made to appear extraordinary in relation to the form and content of its social, political, and historical constitution. These common aspects of everyday life are articulated through language in the practices of 'text' and 'talk'. As an embodiment of 'text' and 'talk', discourse can also be interpreted as a meta-language, and can be a useful focus in textual analysis to demystify a 'mythic language'.

According to Edward Said (1978), "mythic language is discourse" (p. 321). This implies that there is a systematic quality to the ways that myth works in culture and society. As discourse, the production and practice of myth is not necessarily an effect of conscious individual or group agency. The production of myth occurs largely unconsciously and involuntarily through ideology and its manifestations in the institutions that help to order society. This is how the existence of myth, as discourse, is maintained in the process. Narrowing the broad approach of textual analysis to reveal myth in cultural narratives, it is the opinion of this author that critical discourse analysis (CDA) is the best methodology that can be employed towards these ends.

VII. CRITICAL DISCOURSE ANALYSIS

THEORY AND METHODOLOGY REVISITED – From Semiotics to CDA

> *What a man* [sic] *sees depends both on what he looks at and also upon what his previous visual-conceptual experience has taught him to see.*
> (Kuhn, 1962, p. 113)

Critical discourse analysis (CDA) provides an excellent methodology for studying and revealing the ways that myth works within cultural narratives. Similar to the ways that Barthes' (1972, 1984) work extends the field of semiotics by expanding on the work of early semiologists like Saussure (1996a), CDA methods, used by theorists like Bret Dellinger (1995), Teun van Dijk (1998), and Thomas Huckin (n.d.) offer some tools that can be useful to locate myth. By taking a moment to recap the work of these theorists, I intend to highlight the theoretical evolution of the methodology that I plan to employ.

The earlier textual theorists focused on the production of meaning within structured languages. As a linguist, Saussure (1996b) focused primarily on the relations of signs with other signs. He established a theoretical model of signification that focused on the differential relationship of signs as they are composed by parts known as signifier and signified. This model laid the groundwork for studying systems of signs and their meanings. Barthes (1968, 1972, 1984, and 1996) furthered this system of signification, conceptualizing a second-order in the production process of meaning. He primarily focused on studying orders of signification and how meaning is created in the relationship between sign systems and culture. His model examined how meanings were structured within cultural stories through "chains of related concepts" known as myth (Fiske, 1990, p. 88).

Expanding on Barthes' (1972, 1984) work with myth, CDA theorists offer tools that can be useful towards a textual analysis of cultural narratives. In short, CDA incorporates an analysis of the social relations of power that exist, within the formal structures of language, through everyday practices of 'text and talk' (Dellinger, 1995; Huckin, n.d.; Van Dijk, 1998). By analyzing aspects of cultures in their narrative form, cultures, in this sense, can be read as texts and interpreted through speech acts and dialogue. CDA offers a critical reading of cultural texts – and the subsequent dialogue born of these texts – by analyzing the ways in which meanings are articulated, disarticulated, and re-articulated through discourse. In the process, this method also examines the ways in which contested cultural narratives are structured in social relations of power. In order to better understand CDA, a brief description on discourse is necessary at this juncture.

THE ROLE OF DISCOURSE & POWER IN CRITICAL ANALYSIS

Previously described as a sense of cohesion between signs and their meanings, discourse enters as an intermediary between ideology and language. Drawing upon Michel Foucault's (2003) 'strategic model of intelligibility'[17], discourse contextualizes a power dynamic through ideas about an object or concept. Constituted in social interaction, discourse is not merely language – as characterized by the empty signifiers within sign systems. Discourse is a force in itself that functions as a weapon; effectively producing powerful social effects (Foucault, 2003). By virtue of Foucault's conception of

---

17 Discourse as a 'strategic model of intelligibility' refers to the power relations intrinsic to its ontology. These power relations imply an internal logic or 'strategic coherence' that operates beyond formal linguistic structures to analyze how statements function socially as opposed to how they function semantically. (Foucault, 2003, pp. xix-xx)

discourse – as a form of 'strategic intelligibility' – power, therefore, becomes a central notion to critical methods of research that analyze discourse.

Power, according to Teun Van Dijk (1998), is a form of control. Dominant groups, therefore, are defined as such in relation to the control that they effectively exercise over the thoughts and actions of other groups. The other groups that are subjugated, under the control exercised by the dominant, are ultimately subordinated in the interests of maintaining this relationship of power. This is not to say, however, that power is absolute.

Many forms of social control vary, relative to the respective social relationships of privilege that it operates within. Access to specific presupposed bases of social resources like information, money, legislation etc (Van Dijk, 1998) are all resources through which power can be exercised. Coupled with conventions surrounding social interaction, these resources can help to determine the form of power. As a result, various groups may exercise a relative degree of control over others depending on the situation or social domain.

For example, as a professor, Philippe Rushton embodies a form of scholarly power over his lectures. As a professor, it is determined through the conventions of tenure and the academy that his job is to control the information disseminated to the students who participate in his lectures. Within this relationship of power, Rushton subjects his students to the information that he chooses to lecture about. The students do not choose the information that Rushton will lecture about. As a result Rushton exhibits a form of control over the education of his students. This control is exercised as a result of the presupposed expertise that he is believed to possess and is agreed upon through the conventions of his position within the academy.

Although the exercise of power may oftentimes seem explicitly universal – as in common cases of crime and punishment through the rule of law – power, however, is rarely absolute. In order to illustrate this point, it would be useful to expand upon the example using the professor above. Even though professor Rushton can exercise a form of power over his students within a lecture setting, his powers as a professor do not extend far beyond that setting. His powers, regarding access to the information used in his research, become less defined when confronted by the powers of his peers who produce information to refute his research. Moreover, his powers as a psychology professor would have no merit if he were to face criminal charges in a court of law. This illustrates that the type of power exercised is relative to the situational aspects of interaction within the overall social context. Indeed power embodies many forms of social action.

Power can be explicitly embodied through social action, as a judge sentences an offender to time in jail or a president declares war on another country. Power can also be implicitly embodied, in actions guided by everyday social etiquette, common presuppositions, and myth. It is the opinion of this author that the latter embodiment of power, as implicitly formed, is very common yet overlooked, and is therefore most saliently deserving of our attention in the ways that it engenders dominance at the expense of others. In both instances, however, power is exercised, embodied, or committed – intentionally or not – through discourse.

In this sense, discourse is "the unit of actual language use in which power is enacted" as a form of social control (Van Dijk, 1998). Those who are considered to be in a privileged position of dominance are said to exhibit a degree of social control in relation to those who lack the necessary degree of social control and are often subjugated to the will of the dominant. As in the above example, those who exercise more control over discourse – like a professor – can be said to have more power and are, therefore, perceived to be more dominant than those who exercise less control over discourse – like the students in the professor's class. For Van Dijk (1998), "CDA attempts to focus on the *abuse* of such power ... on the ways control over the discourse is abused to control peoples beliefs and actions in the interest of dominant groups, and against the best interests and the will of others". An example of an abuse of power, in this respect, could be seen in the ways in which professor Rushton's control over discourse promoted racist beliefs. For the purposes of this thesis, however, I will be primarily using CDA to focus on the implicit quality of power – the ways it is made to look natural and taken for granted in everyday discourse – as embodied in social myth and manifest through the practices of 'text and talk'.

The practices of 'text and talk' reveal that a multiplicity of discourses exists. These discourses, some of which are contestable or amendable to each other respectively, are only accessible through language. The most common pallets, through which discourse can be dissected, exist in the form of artefacts that can be read as texts. A newspaper article, for example, can be used as an excellent sample artefact to illustrate the ways through which discourse works within a text. It is important to note, however, that although discourse can be analyzed through a critical reading of a newspaper article (Van Dijk, 2000); the power of discourse is not limited to the written word. It also exists in speech, ethics, images, and institutions. CDA, therefore, is primarily concerned with the ways in which power is distributed between individuals and groups, within society, through forms of social exchange. As a central tenet of CDA, a 'context-sensitive' approach to analyzing the social distribution of power is highly ethical in the ways in which its method is ultimately used towards improving society.

According to Huckin (n.d.), the use of CDA pays close attention to "power imbalances, social inequities, non-democratic practices, and other injustices in hopes of spurring readers to corrective action". In its broad outreach towards social justice, this method of analysis locates specific relations of power within an overall social context through which the text and the theorists alike are ultimately situated. Because of this, theorists working with tools from CDA oftentimes make no apologies – and in my opinion rightly so – for the polemical tone of their research. This can perhaps be attributed to a view of discourse, which assumes that people's perception of reality is primarily formed in and through social interaction.

Acknowledging the fact that social interaction is mediated through language, CDA examines the complex power relationship between what the author of the text brings to bear on the production of a message, and what the reader of the text brings when interpreting a message (Dellinger, 1995). This does not imply, however, that power is necessarily distributed equally in any form of social interaction. Recognizing that texts are produced within a social and historical context, the analyst interprets the creators of texts as socially and historically situated subjects, driven by their own ideological agendas. Because of this, members of a dominant group (i.e. professors) consistently construct and communicate dominant versions of reality that effectively work to secure their own interests (i.e. lecture on topics that exclusively support their research). These dominant (research) interests are oftentimes secured at the expense of subjugating the subordinated (research) interests of others. This process, however, is not always as explicit as it may initially sound. Indeed, the interests of the dominant group are often procured in subtle ways that are often taken-for-granted as natural and common-place. A theorist will often use CDA to reveal and make explicit these subtle practices of domination and subjugation, in the interest of siding with the victims of oppression (Huckin, n.d.).

In order to maximize the efficacy of siding with victims of oppression, it is a common goal of the CDA theorists to try and make their work accessible to a large readership. According to Huckin (n.d.), the research produced by these theorists must be as clear as possible, avoiding unnecessary jargon and highly specialized scientific language without sacrificing too much accuracy at the conclusion of analysis. As ideal as this goal may appear, there exists an irony intrinsic to this task, especially within scholarly circles.

To clarify and perhaps expand upon Huckin's (n.d.) proposition, the research produced by theorists working with CDA must be accessible to a *target* readership. Indeed, the theorist's research must not only be relatively accessible but more importantly the theorist must be conscious of an intended readership when producing research. For example, data collected by scholars and academics, if produced for scholarly or academic purposes, must be presented in a commensurate scholarly or academic discourse in order for their research to be seriously engaged by the intended readership. In so doing, the relative success of the message is contingent upon how accurately the encoded objective is decoded by the reader of the message.

Keeping in mind that the theorist is also situated within a larger ideological social context, this relative success can be measured by the degree to which the reader is interpolated by the inscribed ideologies of the text. Although the theorist must employ a similar process of communication used by dominant groups to subjugate subordinated groups, the struggle over meaning is reversed to affect the process' liberating potential. This is usually done by demystifying an appeal to convention through myth.

MYTH, IDEOLOGY, KNOWLEDGE – Multidisciplinary Discursive Approach

Objects and subjects, communicated by convention through myths, are understood in and of themselves to be natural and commonsense. Discourse arms the analyst with a useful conceptual tool to reveal myth by demystifying its commonsensical appeal within the cultural perception of reality. As a result, CDA is useful in analyzing both the form and content of media texts. This creates a broader base for a multidisciplinary approach to textual analysis.

A multidisciplinary approach to CDA contrasts with the notion of ideology as false consciousness. This method perceives ideology as a foundation of interpretive frameworks that organize the attitudes and values of a social group or culture. In contrast to previously held notions, ideologies are not arbitrary beliefs, but specific group systems (Van Dijk, 2002). These systems are organized by cultural characteristics that represent identity, social structure, and the position of the subject or group within an interactive environment. Ideologies are the foundations that determine the content and form of all social representations. This definition of ideology may lead one to believe that knowledge is essentially ideological. According to Van Dijk (2002), however, not all knowledge is ideological.

For Van Dijk (2002) it can be argued that every culture or group relies on a commons of shared, undisputed information that they accept as fact. Knowledge, therefore, is a shared belief, relative to the culture or group in their present state of being, that is socially justified through consensus. Knowledge is a belief that becomes understood as indisputable within the confines of the group. Because of this, shared knowledge is usually assumed to be rooted in the material conditions of existence. In this sense, Van Dijk (2002) considers knowledge to be 'pre-ideological'. Without this notion of knowledge as 'pre-ideological', Van Dijk (2002) believes that groups would not be able to communicate among each other.

Although the concept of 'pre-ideological' knowing makes sense according to the framework theorized by Van Dijk (2002), it is the opinion of this author, however, that no such claims are absolutely accurate in the entirety of their formulations as such. In order for information to be labelled as knowledge, it must involve a cognitive process of interpreting and articulating reality.

According to Ericson et al., "reality is a result of cognitive processes of interpretation, and social processes of construction" (p. 18). These processes cannot be articulated as knowledge before passing through the mechanism of language and cannot be initially conceived before passing through the mechanisms of cognition. As a result, knowledge must essentially be a form of thought. According to Terry Eagleton (1990): "There is no such thing as presuppositionless thought, and to this extent all of our thinking might be said to be ideological" (pp. 3-4).

The form of knowledge that Van Dijk (2002) theorizes can be used interchangeably with Barthes' (1972, 1984) notion of myth. To state this point more explicitly, all knowledge can potentially contain mythic qualities and all myths attempt to articulate some form of knowledge. This being the case, it is impossible then for knowledge to exist beyond ideology simply for the reason that myths – according to Barthes (1972, 1984) – are essentially ideologically loaded, social constructs. Myth essentially works to mask language's ideological foundations through a discourse that decontextualizes an object or subject of all historical contingencies. Knowledge – even that of a scientific pedigree – is contingent upon the cognitive process of interpretation and must be subjected to articulation through a system of language, if it is to be communicated as such. As a result, that which is considered as empirical knowledge can also be susceptible to colonization by myth. For example, using the principle of uncertainty in quantum theory, knowledge cannot be perceived as absolute (Ericson et al, 1987).

Quoting Werner Heisenberg[18], Ericson et al. (1987) emphasizes the relative quality of knowledge in the empirical sciences by stating that: "What we observe is not nature itself, but nature exposed to our methods of questioning" (p. 18). The similarities between myth and knowledge are too glaring to overlook especially in the ways that discourse, as a communicative practice, works among the two concepts. Discourse plays an important role in the way that ideology is perceived and can illustrate that Barthes' (1972, 1984) theory of myth is compatible with Van Dijk's (2002) theory of knowledge.

For Van Dijk (2002), discourse among groups requires a base of common knowledge that is perceived to be free of ideological bias in order to maximize commensurability in communicative action. Although he believes that some knowledge is 'pre-ideological', it essentially boils down to the ways in which ideology is perceived in relative terms, that holds his argument together, and not necessarily how it actually exist in absolute terms. This point is illustrated further when Van Dijk (2002) explains that once shared knowledge is manifest in discourse, and articulated through language, it becomes susceptible to scrutiny from other groups that do not share the same knowledge

---

18 For more information on Werner Heisenberg and the uncertainty principle in quantum theory, please refer to the American Institute of Physic website: <Hhttp://www.aip.org/history/heisenberg/p01.htmH>

base. Outside groups may find such knowledge ideologically biased, leading the perception of knowledge to shift in the same ways that myth shifts when revealed by the analyst. In sum, as knowledge is articulated through language, it automatically becomes subject to a historical context. If history is "ideologically and politically inflected time" (Dellinger, 1995), knowledge – like myth – becomes susceptible to ideological bias when articulated through language in spite of how ideologically neutral it may appear. Knowledge, therefore, is not ideologically neutral.

Articulated through language, knowledge claims are ultimately subject to the same historical context that language is. This leaves meaning open to possible change. Knowledge, in this respect, is evolutionary. Even members of the same group or culture may find knowledge from a previous time period, within their group or culture, ideological. It is important to note however, that although knowledge may be deemed ideological from the standpoint of another culture at another time, it can still be considered knowledge from the perspective of the culture that accepts it as such. This epistemological relationship is referred to as 'relative relativism' (Van Dijk, 2002).

Relativism as a concept is also subject to *relative* critique. Knowledge is always knowledge relative to the perceptions of the respective epistemic community. Once accepted as knowledge within a given culture, in the given temporal context, meaning becomes obvious and taken-for-granted as fact by virtue of convention based on consensus a priori. This taken-for-granted nature is characteristic of Barthes' notion of myth. Once the knowledge of a community is considered a belief by an outside community, the discourse of that knowledge is interpreted as having an ideological bias. In contrast, if the knowledge of a community is deemed to be factual within the said community, the discourse of that knowledge is reflected in the belief systems of that community. This shows the complexity of a multidisciplinary approach to textual analysis when deconstructing cultural narratives through a context-laden, evaluative methodology like CDA.

THE FLEXIBLE QUALITY OF CDA – A Malleable Methodological Approach

As a highly contextual, multidisciplinary approach to textual analysis, CDA offers a broad repertoire of analytic tools that can be used for analysing a number of different cultural artefacts as textual subjects. According to Huckin (n.d.), "not every concept found in a linguistics textbook…is equally useful when it comes to doing critical discourse analysis, and even CDA analysts differ somewhat among themselves in the kinds of tools they employ". Depending on the subject analyzed, the tools of analysis may differ in combination and type. For example, CDA analysts with a strong background in Structural Linguistics may employ tools from semiotics when analyzing the signs and sign systems of a cultural text whereas CDA analysts with a background in Economics may use tools derived from political economy when analyzing the commodification of cultural practices. As a result, "there is no standardized form of CDA methodology" (Huckin, n.d.).

Although there is no consistent form of CDA methodology, there are, however, common elements and objectives that unify CDA as an analytical approach to research methods. Like any other analytical approach to research methodology, CDA employs a wide range of tools to conduct precise analyses as mentioned above. It is at the discretion of the researcher, therefore, in conjunction with the subject being studied, to determine the appropriate tools for analysis that would best suit the thesis being researched. For the purposes outlined in this thesis, I will borrow from some of the tools and analytical approaches used by the aforementioned theorists (Huckin, n.d.; Van Dijk, 1998) that have used CDA to analyze the written texts of newspaper articles.

LEVELS OF ANALYSIS – A Multi-layered Technique

Common to the research conducted using CDA on newspaper articles, are the levels and approaches to reading the text. Van Dijk (1998) draws from some basic concepts of CDA to formulate a theoretical framework that identifies the relationship between discourse, cognition, and society. For Van Dijk, there are at least two levels of reading a text that must be bridged by some basic conceptual tools in order for CDA to be useful as a unified method of analysis. These two levels of analysis include **macro** and **micro** approaches to reading a text.

At the micro level of analysis, the reader is primarily focused on the ways in which meanings are structured within the text itself. This is seen by analysing the use of language and formal aspects of communication as interpreted within a personal and group context. The macro level of analysis deals with notions of power and the ways in which it is distributed among various interpretive communities within society at large. This level focuses on issues of inequality and dominance, inscribed in the text, as it is situated within the broader social context. Although Van Dijk (1998) conceptually formulates these levels of analysis as existing on two separate plains, he makes clear the fact that both these levels of analysis are by no means absolute or mutually exclusive. Both macro and micro levels are present in any common social interaction. This will become more evident through a critical reading of the *Toronto Star's* articles on racial profiling and the larger multicultural context through which the articles are situated. Macro and micro levels of analysis, used by Van Dijk (1998) are similar to the three levels of analysis used by Thomas Huckin (n.d.).

According to Thomas Huckin (n.d.), there are three main levels of analyzing a written text. For Huckin (n.d.) the text is first read as a whole, keeping the possible perspective of the ordinary reader in mind. This is the level where myths are most effectively inscribed within the public psyche as knowledge. Ideological manipulations are more effective at this stage through the types of discourse used. Once the text is recognized and read as a whole – within the formal structures and conventions of a specific genre – the reader can proceed to interpreting the text on a sentence by sentence level.

Reading the text as a collection of separate sentences is the second level from which a text can be analyzed. By reading a text sentence by sentence, the meanings of sentences are constructed to fit within the conventions of the overall genre. This sentence by sentence level of analysis pays close attention to the ways in which sentences are structured into topics that identify and reinforce important meanings. These meanings, reinforced through sentence topic, reveal important ways that bias or perspective is created in the issues reported. Writers often use sentence topics to articulate their bias in their efforts to sway or influence the reader's perspective towards the interests encoded in the text. Once meanings are constructed and interpreted at the sentence level, the reader can proceed to analyzing the text at the level of words and phrases.

The third level of reading texts is the most detailed of all three levels of analysis. Reading a text at the level of words and phrases opens up room to explore additional meanings inscribed in the text. These additional meaning are commonly revealed through tools derived from semiotics. Understanding the orders of signification with tools like denotation, connotation and myth is especially useful when analyzing words and phrases in relation to their broader social and cultural contexts. Although these levels of analysis are specifically used to analyze single news articles, they can be applied broadly in an analysis of an entire news paper series. Bellow are some tools that may be useful for analyzing news paper texts.

TOOLS OF THE TRADE FOR 'TEXT AND TALK'

All of the aforementioned levels of analysis can reveal the pervasiveness of myth as they are hidden within cultural texts. These myths, masquerading as objective knowledge through discourse, can be revealed through tools that assess qualities of the text such as: **framing**, to determine the overall tone, bias, perspective, and conceptual parameters of the news article; **visual aids**, to determine the intentional use of photographs, illustrations, graphs, charts, diagrams, and or font to attract the attention of the reader to certain aspects a news article; **foregrounding** and **back grounding**, to determine an order of emphasis on details and information within a news article; **omissions**, to determine what critical information a news article may be leaving out; **presupposition** and **insinuation**, to determine the ideas or concepts that are taken for granted as facts within a news article; **discursive differences**, to determine the genres and variations of language, as they are to be used to their degree of formality, in a specific social or group context (register) within the news article; **topicalization**, to determine the value of the subject being placed at the beginning of the sentence in a news article, and; **connotation**, to determine the second-order meanings inscribed within the text through metaphors, myths, and metonyms within the news article. All three levels of analysis employ a combination of the analytic tools described above.

Although these tools are useful when analyzing written texts, they are not absolute in their methodological application. As mentioned above, there is no standardized methodology to CDA. As a result, the aforementioned tools are relative to the expertise of the analyst in conjunction with the subject of analysis being considered. These tools form the textual area of analysis, and are in no way conclusive without careful and critical consideration to the overall social, political and historical context of the written document. Once a thorough textual analysis is complete, CDA theorists must sum up their research by providing a "contextualized interpretation" (Huckin, 2002) of their findings. This methodology rejects notions of objective research and value free knowledge claims.

For CDA theorists, knowledge is a product of continually evolving discourses of social interaction. Articulated, disarticulated, and rearticulated through language, knowledge is considered as such, by gaining a relative degree of imagined consistency in its conquest over scrutiny among a contested field of discursive negotiation. As a result, knowledge claims cannot be interpreted as absolute formulations of objective reasoning. Such claims are coded in discourse and validated through myth by virtue of popular and authoritative consensus.

Articulated through language and communication, a dominant conception of knowledge, or myth, is essential to making sense of reality. As a dominant communicative institution, the mass media plays an important role in the production of knowledge and the perpetuation of myths. Likewise, knowledge and myths constitute a form of collective consciousness that is used as a framework through which to interpret reality. Indeed, understanding the role of the mass media in society is crucial to understanding dominant perceptions of reality through a mediated stream of consciousness.

VIII. A MEDIATED STREAM OF CONSCIOUSNESS

REALITY AND THE MEDIA'S PRODUCTION OF PERCEPTION

> *I am an invisible man ... I am invisible, understand, simply because people refuse to see me... That invisibility to which I refer occurs because of a particular disposition of the eyes of those with whom I come in contact. A matter of the construction of the* inner *eyes, those eyes with which they look through their physical eyes upon reality.*
>
> (Ellison, 1947, p. 3)

Reality is constructed in and through communication (Littlejohn, 1996). As a result, reality is agreed upon through language common to a collective community of ideas. This collective community of ideas emerges through perpetual dialogue among competing and negotiating discourses. Because of this, interpretations of reality as a product of discourse, manifest in the production and reproduction of cultural artefacts, are articulated and interpreted through language and can therefore be read as texts. The meanings generated by these texts are created in the negotiation of discourse through social interaction. Meanings are dialogical. And as a result, we are said to live in and through systems of meanings and representations (Shohat & Stam, 1995).

In short, reality is formed in meanings produced by the discourses, negotiated as dominant, that emerge out of our social interactions. These discourses are communicated through systems of representation. Indeed, systems of representation are usually mediated through powerful social institutions. It is the opinion of this author that the mass media are of the most powerful social institutions today, perpetuating dominant discourses that shape popular perceptions of who we are and our notions of reality. As such, the media are socializing forces through which power is exercised and can be seen as dominant institutions of social control (Kellner, 1995a; Real, 1989).

Building upon Wacquant's (2002) thesis, that four 'peculiar institutions' helped to shape racisms in contemporary American society; I would place the mass media as a fifth 'peculiar institution', which works in a similar way to the previous four. To further this claim on the profound role of the media, in providing materials that influence our perceptions of our identities and our world, Douglas Kellner (1995) is worth quoting at length:

> Radio, television, film and the other products of media culture provide materials out of which we forge our very identities, our sense of selfhood; our notion of what it means to be male or female; our sense of class, of ethnicity and race, of nationality, of sexuality, of "us" and "them." Media images help shape our view of the world and our deepest values: what we consider good or bad, positive or negative, moral or evil. Media stories provide the symbols, myths and resources through which we constitute a common culture and through which we insert ourselves into this culture. Media spectacles demonstrate who has the power and who is powerless, who is allowed to exercise force and who is not. They dramatize and legitimate the power of the forces that be and show the powerless that they must stay in their place or be destroyed. (p.5)

As illustrated in the passage cited above, the mass media can be seen as pervasive pedagogical tools that – among other things – teach us: who we are, how to act, and how to interpret our surroundings. Michael Real (1989) neatly sums up the pervasiveness of these institutions in what he calls *super media* that serve "as the central nervous system of modern society" (p. 13). As a constant reminder of the super media's role in shaping and producing collective and individual consciousness, Real (1989) frequently inserts the phrase: 'our media, ourselves' throughout the pages of his book *Super Media*. This illustrates how individual identities blend into media identities in an ongoing dialectic of myth making. Identities, therefore, are not individually produced but are social products developed in and through the mechanisms of language and representation (Turner, 1992). As a result, the *super media* are instrumental to the ways in which meanings are constructed through language and representation. Although the mass media provide us with the tools that we use to organize our existence (reality), a dialectical relationship between the society, individuals and the media, was not always taken into consideration regarding the production of meaning.

MASS MEDIA AND MASS AUDIENCES – Homogeneity to Heterogeneity

Some early theories of the mass media, deriving out of positivistic schools of thought, including instinct psychology, interpreted the notion of the audience as a homogeneous mass (Defleur & Ball-Rokeach, 1989). It was assumed further that this homogeneous mass was uniformly influenced by any message transmitted through the mass media. In this sense, the mass media were, and in some cases still are, perceived as powerful and all pervasive propaganda machines that leave little room for dissenting voices. This implied a perception that a singular universe of ideas formed the basis of an objective reality. As societies became increasingly diverse, however, theories of cultural studies demonstrated that the audience is not a homogeneous mass but a heterogeneous mix of diverse interpretative communities (Agger, 1992; Kellner, 1995; Real, 1989; Turner, 1992).

Through greater focus on the role of language, it became more apparent that various interpretative communities exist, simultaneously, in a multi-verse of ideas. This multi-verse of ideas forms the basis of a subjectively interpreted reality. For Turner (1992), the power of language creates and locates social relations through its own relational systems of representation. As a result, reality is created as relative through the mechanisms of language in culture that sets out to order and define it. Turner (1992) sums up this relation by stating that "culture, as the site where meaning is generated and experienced, becomes a determining, productive field through which social realities are constructed, experienced and interpreted"(p. 15). As logical as this statement may appear, it is the opinion of this author that such a perspective dangerously teeters on the brink of a linguistic determinism, throwing away any claims for a material reality that exists beyond language. Although language offers a strong argument for the discursive construction of meaning, it does not necessarily follow that it creates reality per se. In order to clarify this point, it is worth briefly returning to Stuart Hall (1997).

Hall (1997) states an important distinction between claims that language creates reality, and the claims that language creates meaning in reality. Hall (1997) uses two distinct phrases to illustrate his point. The first phrase, "nothing meaningful exists outside of discourse" is more accurate than the second phrase that states "nothing exists outside of discourse". These statements illustrate Hall's (1996) distinction between linguistic and discursive interpretations of reality. While language and discourse are very powerful agents of culture, they do not take away from the fact that there are real historical and material conditions that form the basis of reality. Of great interest to Hall (1996, 1997) are the ways in which the historical and material conditions of reality are interpreted as meaningful within diverse interpretative communities. By stating that the only way to understand the world is through representation by no means implies that the world only exists through representation.

UNIVERSE AND OR MULTIVERSE – A Many Sided Reality

Communicated through systems of representation, reality is interpreted as a social, cultural, and historical concept experienced and understood in and through discourse. Discourse, as a culturally contingent practice, allows for multiple interpretations of reality to exist simultaneously. This relationship is oftentimes misperceived by some cultural studies theorists in their beliefs that multiple realities exist. A multi-verse is an interpretative condition and is by no means absolute. This can be misleading when analysing the power of the media in society.

The interpretation that multiple realities exists, does not presuppose that power is concentrated primarily in the actions and interpretations of the audience and that the media have superficial effects that are only symbolic within the subjective interpretation of the reader. Communications, and therefore the media, are intrinsically linked with power. This power, intrinsic to the media, has the potential to effect real historical and material conditions on the populations that participate in them by virtue of their socializing mechanisms. Furthermore, understanding that communication is linked with power (Hall, 1997), all interpretations or perceptions of reality are not considered equal.

ACTIVE AUDIENCE AND THE POWER OF MEDIA – Negotiated Dominance

Kellner (1995) warns against placing too much emphasis on an 'active audience' theory, in the interests of maintaining the fact that the media have very 'powerful manipulative effects'. For Kellner (1995), cultural artefacts are situated within ideologically loaded relations of production and reproduction. These ideological relations essentially position cultural forms by the way of either perpetuating or resisting dominance or oppression. This occurs as a result of the discursive process of competition and negotiation where dominant perceptions of reality persist in contention with negotiated and oppositional perceptions of reality (Hall, 1995, 1996, 1997, 2002). Reality, therefore, is a fractured, interchangeable, and fluid contested terrain. Reality is what this author considers to be *negotiated potentiality*.

As dominant discourses emerge, in the negotiation of dominant interpretations of reality, the ideologies implicit to its formation serve to fix the dominant discourse as absolute. This attempt at fixing meaning through discourse makes the dominant interpretation of reality appear to be natural. Indeed, as contingent as reality is, these dominant perceptions remain highly influential in the ways that audiences make sense of the world around them through myth.

Myth naturalizes objects and subjects that become encoded into cultural texts as knowledge claims. Some of these knowledge claims stand out in culture as a form of conceptual and ideological shorthand. As contextual as reality is, when interpreted through forms of communication and representation like language, power intervenes in the interest of fixing meanings as absolute and natural (Hall, 1997). And although reality exists in a multi-verse of interpreted ideas, myths contain a universe of ideological assumptions that exist through the practice of discourse. Indeed, dominant perceptions of reality that monopolize media messages constitute what James Winter (2002) terms *MediaThink*.

Based on George Orwell's 'prevailing orthodoxy of ideas' and continuing in the tradition of the 'propaganda model' (Achbar & Wintonick, 1992; Chomsky, 2002; Herman & Chomsky, 1988; Podur, 2002), *MediaThink* embodies the dominant perspective of reality as perceived through the minds of those who control the media (representatives of a dominant class). It is important to note, however, that dominant perspectives are by no means uniform or absolute. In the competitive process of constant discursive negotiation, there are often cracks and fissures in myth that allow for alternative perspectives to emerge. In this process however, alternative perspectives are often marginalized and or silenced altogether, constantly losing to the overpowering presence of the dominant perspectives (Podur, 2002; Winter, 2002). Furthermore, in very rare circumstances, dominant perspectives can temporarily shift appearing to embrace and incorporate alternative perspectives as a part of the dominant discourse. This is sometimes seen in more 'liberal', popular media sources. Accompanied by a relative amount of backlash, this shift is usually marginal and does not end up straying too far from deeper layers of dominant ideologies that remain entrenched in its overall message. As we will see, this is demonstrated in the *Toronto Star's* coding of 'race' in their coverage of racial profiling.

IX. ANALYSIS OF INCORPORATED RESISTENCE

CONSERVATIVE IDEOLOGIES AND THE LIBERAL MEDIA

The white man is sealed in his whiteness.
The black man in his blackness.

(Fanon, 1967, p. 9)

Although the *Toronto Star's* groundbreaking expose on racial profiling, practiced by the Toronto Police Service (TPS), appears to be critical of racism on a surface reading, a critical reading of selected articles from its series on 'Race and Crime' indicates that despite its best intentions, its coverage of the issues actually serves to propagate racist narratives. These racist narratives are a culmination of the deep rooted sentiments of a colonialist ideology that has evolved to a current state of unquestioned normalcy. Naturalized through 'official' multiculturalism's 'liberal' discourse of tolerance and diversity, *The Star's* normalized brand of racism has been incorporated within the overall language of divisiveness and oppression that it so stridently attempts to eradicate. Its underlying message continues to bear the 'strange fruit' of racist ideologies that undermine attempts at significant change towards social justice and equality. In order to examine this perception further, a textual analysis, considering Barthes' notion of myth through some of tools derived from CDA will be used to explore racism, as a systemic way of life, institutionalized through myth within Canada's multicultural society. Moreover, I will be applying these theories to the ways in which 'race' is coded in *The Star's* coverage of racial profiling as practiced by the TPS.

CDA – An Applied Methodology

As outlined in an earlier chapter of this thesis, tools from CDA can be equally useful when analyzing news stories both in series and as individual articles. Usually when there is enough information and interest (corporate and or public) to publish a number of stories on a particular subject or issue, common themes can be linked to group these stories into a series. As a result an entire series can be read in similar ways to a single article. This chapter will apply some of the tools from CDA, discussed in a previous chapter of this thesis, to a broad analysis of some of the major themes in selected articles from *The Star's* series 'Race and Crime'. Once the common themes about 'race' are analyzed within its broader social context on a macro level, a more specific analysis of excerpts from five selected articles, published as a part of the series, will be analyzed semantically on a micro level.

When conducting a macro reading of *The Star's* coverage of racial profiling as a series, it appears on the surface that the newspaper is attempting to perform its role as the 'fourth estate'. The 'fourth estate' is a term that positions the mass media as a 'watchdog' to government or 'state' abuses of power (Winter, 2002, p. ix). In this case, the police service functions as an extension of the government or state apparatus that works to enforce its laws on the public. In so doing, however, it has become commonly perceived by marginalized voices in Toronto that the practices of law enforcement agencies have become selective to the point of discrimination (Ontario Human Rights Commission, 2003). As a result public trust in the police service – as an extension of government – has been violated by the unjust practice of racial profiling that an organization like the TPS carries out. Under these circumstances, the erstwhile 'liberal' news media, as 'watchdogs' for the public interest against the state's abuses of power, had a duty and responsibility to the public to report on the issues. In this case, it can be argued that *The Star's* coverage on racial discrimination practiced by the TPS is purely responsible journalism in the way that it appears to take a position against the agents of power (TPS) in the racial profiling debate. However, something is missing in this assumption involving the broader role of racism and the mass media in society.

If we will briefly recall from an earlier section of this thesis, the mass media have a relatively large role in the socialization of the status quo – being a consciousness producing industry (Ericson et al., 1987; Kellner, 1995; Real, 1989). Moreover, the media have been highly theorized as a form of social control (Ericson et al., 1987). On a surface reading, *The Star's* coverage of racial profiling appears to counter this assumption about the media. A more critical reading of *The Star's* coverage, however, reinforces the claim that posits the media as a form of social control in the ways in which it reports the issues. Although *The Star* ostensibly appears to side with the victims of oppression, it nonetheless propagates distorted perceptions of 'racial' differences that can be used to further segregate society.

In an October 20th 2002 article titled "Police target black drivers", *The Star* investigative team reported on the issues of racial profiling by using statistics based on rigid categories of 'race' (see Appendix I). According to the investigative team[19]:

> Almost 34 per cent of all drivers charged with out-of-sight violations were black, in the group where race was listed. Yet according to the latest census figures, Toronto's black community represents just 8.1 per cent of the city's population. By contrast, 62.7 percent of Toronto's population is white, but whites account for 52.1 per cent of the motorists charged with out-of-sight traffic offences. (p. A9)

Although the example above highlights a case study of racial discrimination, it further perpetuates distorted notions of difference in the process. A closer look at the

---

[19] *The Star* investigative team that headed up the coverage on racial profiling consisted of : Jim Rankin, Jennifer Quinn, Michelle Shephard, John Duncanson, and Scott Simmie. A full archive of related stories can also be found by visiting the following *Toronto Star* website:
<Hhttp://www.thestar.ca/NASApp/cs/ContentServer?pagename=thestar/Render&=Page&cid =1034935301156H>

example above demonstrates that racial lines drawn between different populations in society can be reduced to 'black' and 'white'. Indeed, Toronto is depicted as a segregated city that is divided between people perceived as 'black' and people perceived as 'white'. As a result, *The Star's* use of rigid racial categories reinforces dominant distortions of 'race', contributing to the racial socialization of the public in the process. It is a distortion, however, to imply that such rigid categorizations exist according to popularly perceived notions of 'race'. As discussed earlier in this thesis, it is problematic to assume that the entire populations can be reduced to 'races' that are either 'black', 'white' or 'other'. This is problematic primarily because such rigid categorizations of 'race' do not neatly correlate to nature as it is implied. Nowhere does the above statement address the issues of 'race' as an imaginary attribute of racialization nor does it address the effects of racialization on progressive social relations.

Although *The Star* convincingly exposes the existence of racial profiling, it does little to report on the underlying causes of racism as a way of life that fuel racist practices. As a popular part of one of society's dominant 'peculiar institutions', whose role is to watch the power brokers so to speak, should not a part of this responsibility also entail greater care when reporting on the issues that could potentially affect positive social relations? As a result, it is the opinion of this author that *The Star's* expose on racial profiling is not only incomplete but is also negligent in its social responsibility to accurately inform the public. To clarify what I mean by negligent, *The Star's* coverage continues to reify dominant discourses about 'race' while outright ignoring processes of racialization that enable it to do so in such a normalized fashion.

An earlier chapter of this thesis reveals that *The Star* is aware that 'race' is a scientifically useless construct for categorizing populations of people. Despite this awareness, it continues to publish articles that sensationalize social differences along the lines of 'race'. Many years have passed between *The Star's* coverage on Philippe Rushton, and the genetic studies disproving the scientific existence of 'race', however, what remains the same is the Star's coding of racial difference. It is my contention that if *The Star* were to critically explore the deep structures of racialization, there would be no buffer to prevent its analysis from turning on itself as another organization where racism can be found. In a series that spans at least four months of coverage, *The Star* appears content to immerse itself within the sensationalized debate on whether or not racial profiling exists.

EXISTENCE OF RACIAL PROFILING – Does it Occur in TPS Practices?

Cognizant or unaware, not only do arrest statistics speak volumes about the social reality of racial profiling as a systemic form of racism (Friendly, 2002; Podur, 2002) but so does personal testimony (Ontario Human Rights Commission, 2003). Even for those who find *The Star's* research methodology to be unscientific and inconclusive, the practice of racial profiling by the TPS is still a plausible assumption to say the least (Melchers, 2003).

Racial profiling exists, and I intend to move beyond this claim to shift focus from the overt racist actions of individuals within the institution (a few bad apples as they are often referred to) and concentrate on exploring the more subtle nuances of racisms that are produced and produce such individuals within the institution itself. In so doing, it has become evident that institutional forms of racisms – as seemingly invisible products of a deep seated socialization that is internalized in the everyday policies, practices, and silence – directly and/ or indirectly contribute to more visible overt acts of discrimination and inequality (Wise, 1999). This is evidenced by the ways in which *The Star's* own subtle racism is overlooked in their accusations that the TPS is an overtly racist organization. This is further compounded in the TPS reaction to *The Star's* accusations that systemic racism exists within their organization.

Although an organization like the TPS denies systemic racism based on the flawed logic that their policies prevent such acts, the fact that these policies perpetuate the myth that distinct 'races' exist in our multicultural society eludes critical scrutiny. As discussed earlier, if 'race' is an attribute of racism (Darder & Torres, 2004), then the very policies erected by the TPS to protect citizens from racial profiling are essentially racist and therefore institutionalized. Furthermore, these policies are used to identify racism as individual acts carried out through isolated occurrences and do not examine the systemic qualities of racism overall. Due to the narrow reasoning and understanding of racisms within TPS policy, it becomes almost impossible for the TPS to see that they are a racist institution because the logic of their internal policies negates the possibility that such a form of systemic discrimination can even exist. It can be said, therefore, that sometimes the policies which are created to protect against racial discrimination end up perpetuating the existence of separate 'races' as natural. Discussed in an earlier chapter of this thesis, a clear example of this is seen through the notion of 'official multiculturalism' in Canada. As a result, 'race' becomes reified, narrowing the possibilities of racisms to individual and organizational practices while ignoring the subtleties intrinsic to its systemic form as a way of life. In this instance, institutional racisms not only becomes perceived as impossible for the TPS but also becomes overlooked in *The Star's* coverage of the TPS discriminatory practices.

Like the TPS, *The Star's* coverage of racial profiling reifies 'race' as a natural factor, without giving attention to the process of racialization that normalizes a dominant discourse about 'race'. A clear example of this can be seen in the previous section of this chapter. Indeed, racisms are more than just practiced. They are lived through myth and discourse. As can be seen in the selected headlines and articles that follow, *The Star's* coverage merely targets the actions of individuals within the institution without fully analysing the racist structures of the institution itself that produces these individuals and their respective actions. As a result its coverage alludes to systemic racisms without critically engaging in the debate about systemic racism and what it means to society as a whole.

In a March 18th 2003 article titled "Singled out", *The Star's* investigative team reports that: "The Toronto crime data also shows a disproportionate number of black motorists are ticketed for violations that only surface following a stop. This difference ... suggests police use racial profiling in deciding whom to pull over" (p. A1). This information alludes to systemic racism as the organized actions of members within an institution that single out citizens based on notions of 'race'. This, however, merely addresses the practice of racism without challenging the broader social lifestyle that enables the practice. The practice of racial profiling is only one aspect of systemic racism. It does not address all the issues necessary to eradicate racism from society. As a result, *The Star* only addresses the fact that certain citizens are targeted for criminal activity based on perceived racial differences. It does not address the depth and scope of racism as a way of life within society. In the process, systemic racism is made to look as a though it is a simple matter of police abuses of power. *The Star's* coverage does little beyond this report to expose the underlying social structures, engendering racist ways of life, which impel racist actions – individual or collective.

Although *The Star* appears to acknowledge that racisms exists beyond the individual acts practiced by 'a few bad apples' within an organization, it still does not present a clear depiction of the depth and scope of systemic racisms as a way of life. As depicted in the example above, *The Star's* understandings of systemic racisms are merely conflated from the actions of individuals to the practices of an entire organization that can be as one 'bad apple' organization. By focusing on the racist practices of the TPS, *The Star's* narrow view of systemic racism excludes its own practices from critical scrutiny. Indeed, its accusations of the overtly racist practices of the TPS serves to mask the more subtle racisms found in the discourse of its own coverage.

Both *The Star's* evasion of its own racisms and the TPS denial of racisms among its ranks, exist as testaments to the pervasive quality of institutional racisms that exists within the myth of a multicultural society that is rooted in colonialist ideologies. Being so immersed and consumed within the ideologies of the dominant myths about 'race' makes it hard to realize the ubiquitous systems of oppression that serve to sustain the dominant relations of power through the process of racialization. As a result racisms are not always a conscious practice and it is not always recognized due to its subtleties within a normalized discourse about 'race'.

As evidenced by the way myths work through normalized discourse, acts of racism are not necessarily predicated on conscious intent. Entire organizations and institutions can practice and live racisms without being consciously aware. As long as the possibility of a subconscious collective agency continues to be negated, systemic 'racisms' will not only remain difficult to prove but also impossible to eradicate. In the case of the TPS response to allegations of racial profiling, denial has been the preferred way of dealing with social anomie. The TPS has denied allegations of racial profiling to the extent that the Toronto Police Association tried to sue *The Star* for libel.

In a June 25th 2003 article, *The Star's* legal affairs reporter, Tracey Tyler, reported that an Ontario Superior Court judge had dismissed "a $2.7 billion class action libel lawsuit brought against the Toronto Star". The Toronto Police Association had filed the lawsuit claiming that *The Star's* series on 'Race and Crime' implied that all members of the TPS were "racists" thus tarnishing the reputation of every officer on the force. The lawsuit was dismissed on the grounds that it there was no "reasonable cause of action" (p. A1). While the TPS took legal action to deny their practices of overt racisms, *The Star's* more subtle racisms can be found throughout its coverage on the issues.

The Star's subtle forms of racism can be found in its incomplete expose of institutional racisms. By focusing on overt racist actions practiced by the TPS, *The Star* essentially avoids the more subtle racisms innate to the way that they report on such acts. As a result, I will not engage in the debate about whether racial profiling exists, but I will, however, examine the power dynamic intrinsic to these debates through myth generated about common notions of 'race'. In so doing, the focus of this analysis turns to the more subtle and systemic racisms practiced by the *Toronto Star*.

As mentioned above, *The Star* is not exempt from the grasp of institutionally racist practices. This becomes apparent from a closer examination of the ways in which 'race' is coded in the language of its texts. For the purpose of textual analysis, I am more concerned with the type of socio-political assumptions imbedded in the language of a commonsense racial discourse. More specifically, I am interested in the ways that myths about 'race' are perpetuated within our commonly held assumptions about it. By examining the ways in which *The Star* perpetuates a common discourse about 'race', the depth of racisms through myth becomes particularly revealing. As a result, close attention is paid to the ways that myth incorporates the *Toronto Star's* seemingly radical coverage of racial profiling within the dominant ideological framework about 'race'. These myths that fuel common perceptions about 'race', as seen through the *Toronto Star's* coding of racial difference, present a unique and perhaps startling perspective that delves deeper into the roots of racisms as a systemic problem, couched in a racist colonial discourse and appropriated within the 'liberal' ideologies of difference as it is institutionalized and tolerated within a Canadian 'multicultural' environment.

COLOUR-CODED – Visualizing 'Race' and the Perpetuation of Myth

In the *Toronto Star's* series on 'Race and Crime', 'race' is represented through skin colour and crime becomes racialized only when people of colour are involved in the discussion[20]. In this case, the language of 'race' used to expose and resist the dominant ideology of oppression, unwittingly shares a common myth about 'race' as practiced through a common racial discourse signified through colour. These representations of 'race' reinforce a dominant myth about 'race' by utilizing a mythic language about 'race'.

Invoking some of the aspects of ideology discussed early on in this thesis, Fiske (1990) articulates the concept of incorporation. According to Fiske (1990), incorporation

---

20 For more on how crime is racialized, see the *Znet* articles written by Tim Wise. In these articles Wise lists many acts of deviance commonly committed by people perceived as 'white'. For the most part, when regarding the crimes committed almost exclusively by 'whites', 'race' does not appear to be a factor nor does it appear to be a cause for concern. For example, 'race scientists' like Philippe Rushton and neo-conservatives like Dinesh D'Souza, do not *race* to prove a genetic or cultural deficiency that can be generalized to the entire group of people perceived as 'white'. For crimes committed by people perceived to be grouped by colour, however, 'race' becomes treated as a causal factor for deviance. This shows that a colour-blind discourse links 'whiteness' with individuality whereas 'colour' or 'blackness' designates group generalities. Discussed throughout this thesis, racist perspectives that attempt to draw connections between 'race' and crime are reflective of our deeper social consciousness. A colour-blind discourse is also evident in the notion of 'official multiculturalism' in Canada as illustrated through the 'mosaic' metaphor.

accounts for the ways in which "the dominant classes take elements of resistance from the subordinate and use them to maintain the status quo, rather than to challenge it" (p. 181). This demonstrates how aspects of *The Star's* coverage on racial profiling can be hegemonic while at the same time maintaining the appearance of being counter-hegemonic. This can occur when the avenues of resistance contradict a dominant framework through a common discourse. When this happens, elements of resistance can become susceptible to incorporation within the dominant framework, thus robbing the text of a radical voice. In this case, *The Star's* attempt at resistance is incorporated within the dominant framework about 'race' through practising a shared discourse that is supported through the common language of colour-coding. As a result, resistance and dominance become equally intelligible through the utilization of the same language about 'race'. This epitomizes the process of hegemony at its best.

Through the process of hegemony, elements of resistance that are historically and culturally produced in social relations of power are susceptible to inoculation into the culture of the majority by the dominant minority. Discussed in a previous chapter of this thesis, inoculation is one of Barthes' (1984) rhetorical forms of myth. As a result, the subordinate surrenders to the will of the dominant by consent and further perpetuates dominant meanings as they become produced in social relations of power. Moreover, resistant forces are positioned, a priori, by virtue of the shared meanings produced by the dominant in these social relations of power, to articulate and perpetuate their own means of subordination and oppression. Focusing on the language within a text, as well as its social implications, colour-coding calls on the readers to adopt and accept dominant positions that lead us to believe there are fixed and clearly delineable racial differences among us.

Throughout *The Star's* coverage on racial profiling, 'race' is never directly defined. It is alluded to through skin colour classification, as a part of the dominant myth; it is assumed as obvious that 'race' is based primarily on physical appearance. Despite its racist implications rooted in a racist science (as discussed in a previous chapter of this thesis regarding Philippe Rushton), skin colour, therefore, becomes the prominent signifier of 'race'. In order to clarify this relationship, let us examine the process and orders of signification as they relate to the mythic sign 'black'.

'Black' as a sign, constructed within a process of signification, is robbed of its historical and political context once myth takes hold of it. As myth colonizes the sign 'black', it emerges fully developed as a statement of fact and appears to have meaning all by itself. Seeing that the sign has been colonized by myth, its significance is made appear eternal. 'Black' as a sign related to the concept of 'race', for instance, appears as though it has always been a natural designation of difference along the lines 'blackness' which is culturally related to skin colour. This however, is a distortion of history. Examples of this can be seen in a previous chapter of this thesis that outlines shifting histories of 'race'. Indeed, this history has been obscured and the sign 'black', when used in common discourse, has been emptied of any political significance. Myth makes 'black' look natural, by ignoring its cultural significance.

Umberto Eco (1996) speaks about how cultures condition the colours we see. The interpretation of colour is a cultural matter. According to Eco (1996), the "content of a signification system depends on our cultural organization of the world into categories" (p. 155). Notions of 'black' and 'white' are cultural categories used to designate difference within a sea of relational differences. When colour is used as a designation of 'race', it becomes one of many signifiers that float within this sea of relational differences. For instance, the name 'black' – as a signifier – has no exact colour content. It is a label that is arbitrary and empty. It becomes fixed by the meanings attributed to it through a network of relational differences that provoke a mental concept about it. For example, the signifier 'black' provokes a concept of 'blackness' that it signifies. It gains significance once it becomes inserted into culture where meanings surrounding the sign 'black' is opened up to a second-order of signification. Indeed, colour must be viewed within the context of the interacting semiotic system through which it bears significance.

Colours are semiotic devices that are communicated through the process of signification. As a result colours are not physical pigments in and of themselves but expressions correlated to culturally appropriated units. This is how they become strongly categorized. *The Star* uses colour as already categorized and meaningful in and of itself without acknowledging that it represents notions of 'race' that are situated within a chain of related concepts. 'Black' as a sign of 'race' is written and spoken in ways in which it appears to be a fixed and naturalized category robbed of political, social, and cultural significance. It appears to have meaning all on its own without any cultural context. This is how 'black' is used within *The Star's* coding of racial difference. This occurs when myth captures and eternalizes the object signified, through the orders of signification.

The mental concept created within the first-order of signification is conjoined with other mental concepts invoked from the second-order of signification. These concepts are then combined, constituting 'a chain of related concepts'. Myth colonizes the sign 'black' by eternalizing and naturalizing a notion of 'blackness'. Once colonized, 'black' triggers a chain of related concepts can be seen through the ways in which myth conjures notions of 'blackness' as a 'race' of people who have 'dark skin' and are 'culturally different' from 'white'. It is important to mention, however, Barthes' (1972, 1984) notion that myth does not falsify the truth but distorts it.

If we take 'black' as a signifier that designates 'blackness' to a 'race' of people, this is not an outright false claim in the way in which difference among groups of people are categorized and ordered in the world. It does however distort the ways in which this method of categorization can be interpreted as a natural fact. For example, there are no 'black' races with respect to the significance of 'blackness' bearing any physical correlation to a shade on a colour spectrum. There are however, groups of people who are racialized as 'black' and therefore personify a notion of 'blackness'. Even at this level, myth still tries to accomplish a natural and absolute resolution to this assertion by letting 'black' stand on its own. As discussed in detail throughout the thesis, what constitutes 'race' is a highly contested terrain of shifting significance. Despite this notion, the use of the sign 'black' to refer to a 'race' of people is still quite common, especially in *The Star*.

The use of skin colour, to group differences among a population, is deeply rooted within a myth about 'race' that has been widely proliferated throughout the everyday aspects of society. Grouping one another according to skin colour has become a trademark signifier of our socialization within racist frameworks. Throughout the articles published in the *Toronto Star's* series on 'Race and Crime' the text reveals that: the police use skin colour to identify assailants as seen in arrest records databases (CIPS); *The Star* uses skin colour to refer to groups, or communities of citizens, victimized by TPS practices, and; individual citizens and community groups use the same skin colour descriptors to identify themselves in relation to others.

Skin colour is disguised through myth and is presented as pre-ideological social knowledge. This becomes clear through a micro analysis of the semantic features of excerpts taken from specific *Toronto Star* articles on 'race' and crime. The tools from Huckin's (n.d.) CDA methodology, combining both sentence level and word/ phrase levels of analysis, can be used to conduct Van Dijk's (1998) micro reading of the text. I have taken the liberty of highlighting the key words and phrases in bold text to better illustrate my point.

1) Police target **black** drivers. Star Analysis of traffic data suggests racial profiling. – October 20th 2002.

   Black drivers confronted by the flashing lights of a police cruiser often worry if they're being pulled over for the **colour** of their **skin** ... Police traffic offence data, obtained and analysed by The Star, shows a disproportionate number of **blacks** ticketed for violations that routinely surface only after a stop has been made ... Toronto's police services board has ordered its officers not to analyse raw **race**-based crime **data**, arguing racists might use the resulting statistics to stigmatize ethnic communities. Police follow that rule, and don't record **race** statistics for the purpose of **ethnic analysis**. They do, however, list **skin colour** in most arrest reports when describing a person charged. Its routine in arrests for major crimes, while a record of **skin colour** occurs less often for simple traffic offences ... An analysis of more than 7,500 out-of-sight violations found that **skin colour** was listed in about two-thirds of cases where drivers were ticketed with only this type of offence. And **black drivers** were carrying a heavy load of charges. Almost 34 percent of all drivers charged with out-of-sight violations were **black**, in the group where race was listed. Yet, according t the last census figures, Toronto's **black community** represents just 8.1 percent of the city's population. By contrast, 62.7 percent of Toronto's population is **white**, but **whites** account for 52.1 percent of the motorists charged with out-of-sight traffic offences ... More than a dozen young **black Torontonians** shared their experiences with Star reporters. (October 20th 2002)

2) Racial bias 'a reality': Eves. Premier backs talks on treatment of **blacks** by police. – October 23rd 2002

   The investigation showed **blacks** charged with simple drug possession received harsher treatment than **whites** facing the same charge, and that the disproportionate number of **blacks** were ticketed for offences that would come to light only after a traffic stop was made – a pattern consistent with racial profiling. (October 23rd 2002)

3) **Black leaders** want a say. Not consulted on Dubin move, they charge. – October 26th 2002

Black community leaders say they should have been consulted before the Toronto police Chief Julian Fantino announced a review of the force's **race relations practices** that was prompted The Star's stories on **racial profiling** ... The move follows Star stories that analyzed a police database recording more than 480,000 incidents. It concluded that **blacks** charged with simple drug possession received harsher treatment than **whites** facing the same charge and that a disproportionate number of **blacks** were ticketed for offences that would come to light only after a traffic stop was made – a pattern consistent with **racial profiling**. (October 26th 2002)

4) **Black** arrest rates highest. – October 30th 2002.

A Star investigation, conducted by analyzing police arrest records, showed that in certain cases where police have discretion to use personal judgement, **blacks** receive harsher treatment than **whites**. Last weekend's stories prompted by a flood of letters and phone calls from **black readers** who say they have been subjected to **racial bias** by police ... The same analysis of a police database also reveals that a disproportionate number of **blacks** were charged with **violent crimes** ... The data show that **accused black people** represent nearly 27 percent of the all violent charges; this, although the latest census figures show that only 8.1 percent of the population lists their **skin colour** as **black** ... The Toronto police database contains information on 800,000 criminal and other charges that were laid between 1996 and early 2002 and was obtained under a Freedom of Information request. It lists **skin colour** in nearly 95 percent of **violent cases**. The data show that people with **white skin**, who in the 1996 census says make up 62.7 percent of the population, were underrepresented – accounting for 52.2 percent of the violent charges. People classified as having "**brown**" **skin** accounted for 15.9 percent of the charges, while those in the "**other**" category were charged with 5 percent of violent offences. In most cases "**brown**" is used to refer to people of **South Asian** descent while "**other**" mainly represents people of **Chinese** and other **Far Eastern** origin. (October 30th 2002)

5) Singled out. Star analysis of police crime data shows justice is different for **blacks** and **whites**. – March 18th 2003.

Blacks arrested by Toronto police are treated more harshly than **whites**, a Toronto Star analysis of crime data shows. **Black people**, charged with simple drug possession, are taken to police stations more often than **whites** facing the same charge. Once at the station, accused **blacks** are held overnight, for a bail hearing, at twice the rate of **whites**. The Toronto crime data also shows a disproportionate number of **black motorists** are ticketed for violations that only surface following a traffic stop. This difference, say civil libertarians, community leaders and criminologists, suggests police use **racial profiling** in deciding whom to pull over ... The finding provide hard evidence of what **blacks** have long suspected – **race matters** in **Canadian society** especially when dealing with police ... But **Toronto's black community** has long worried about being **singled out** by police – especially its young **black men** ... To measure differences in treatment of **blacks** and **whites**, The Star focused on Toronto's more than 10,000 arrests for simple drug possession over the six year period. Most people arrested on this charge – 63.8 percent – were **classified by police** as being **white**. About a quarter – 23.6 percent – were **described** as **black**. Remaining **skin colour classifications** in the database are "**brown**" and "**other**." In most cases "**brown**" is used to refer to people of **South Asian** descent while "**other**" mainly represents people of **Chinese** and other **Far Eastern** origin. Together, these **racial categories** accounted for barely 12 percent of simple drug possession charges, and analysis showed that "**browns**" were released in much the same way as whites, while "**others**" were treated more like **blacks** ... And six years of internal police records show their decision to has often fallen harder on **blacks** than on **whites** ... The Star analysis of the police traffic data shows a disproportionate number of **blacks** charged compared to **whites**. (March 18th 2003)

If we recall some of the tools outlined from CDA, foregrounding is a technique that can highlight an object, bringing it to the reader's attention. The articles above illustrate methods of foregrounding on two levels. Foregrounding can set the tone of the entire article through visual aids and can also set the tone of a single sentence through topicalization. When analyzing these headlines through topicalization – a form of foregrounding at the sentence level (Huckin, n.d.) – it is no accident that 'race' identifies the topic or subject of the sentence and ultimately sets the tone for the entire article. In this case, skin colour as a signifier of 'race' is presupposed or insinuated to be a natural factor that is taken-for-granted as connoting cultural difference. These headlines reflect the tenor of stories that report on abuses of 'state' power within a society perceived as naturally segregated. These abuses of 'state' power are reported as the actions carried out by individuals within a purportedly racist organization. This method of foregrounding is further compounded in the style and size of font used as a visual aid.

According to Richard Ericson et al. (1987), "visualization – making something visible to the mind even if it is not visible to the eye – is the essence of journalism." (p.4). Visual aid as a method of foregrounding can be used in at least two ways. It can be used implicitly, through the font size and style of headlines, to capture the reader's attention. It can also be used explicitly, through the use of photographs, charts, diagrams and graphs to affect a more direct result.

The use of graphs as a visual aid can be found in both the first and fifth articles. These graphs are tools of foregrounding used by editorial staffs that help the reader to visualize the point that *The Star* is trying to make. In both of these articles, the graphs illustrate the disparity between 'black' and 'white' citizens as they are represented in the sample of arrest statistics analyzed. These statistics are communicated in a formal register that is discursively framed under the guise of objective scientific authority. When communicated in a formal register, supported by the frame of a positivistic discourse, the data collected can be interpreted and qualified as indisputable fact. It can be further assumed from these graphs that society can be unquestionably categorized in terms of racial difference as naturally observed phenomena. Complementing the use of graphs is the use headlines that attempt to reinforce the assumption that racial difference is absolute and natural.

Headlines of the news articles are always placed in a larger bold font to grab the reader's attention. This is seen in all five examples of *The Star's* coverage on 'race' and crime used above. The large bold fonts of headlines are usually the first thing that the reader sees when scanning the newspaper for stories. Indeed, 'race' as a natural factor is given priority and is taken-for-granted as a natural fact. This grabs the reader's attention from the outset by not only appealing visually to their senses, but by appealing to them textually in the shared meanings of a normalized discourse about 'race'. By just reading the descriptors of skin colour in the headlines, 'race', as a natural way of designating group difference is insinuated. Although *The Star* intentionally grabs the reader's attention through headlines that call attention to racist practices, its own racism is masked through what they choose to omit within the text of the articles selected.

Omitted from the headlines are the ways in which the TPS contribute to the racialization of difference through their practices of racial profiling. In the process of omitting these details, *The Star* further perpetuates the racialization of difference by foregrounding categories of 'race' as a natural group distinction. Because of this omission, all that the reader is called upon to take from the articles are that 'blacks' are victimized by the police because they are naturally different in skin complexion and culturally different in world view. It is important to recall that this difference is coded in relation to an ideal concept of what constitutes sameness. In this case – according to the ideologies that constitute the 'mosaic' metaphor – sameness is equivalent to that which would embody the notion of an ideal Canadian. This illustrates some of the more subtle ways in which racism is perpetuated through myth. As a result, *The Star* further spreads this myth by contributing to the same process of racialization that the TPS is accused of practising. Illustrated by the discourse of these headlines, *The Star* subscribes to the same myth that works to detach the meaning of 'race' from its historical context while masking the ideologies at work that produce its meaning.

Described at length in earlier chapters of this thesis, 'race', as defined through skin colour, has an historical and ideological context that is masked behind a commonsense discourse. This discourse naturalizes power relations through the use of everyday language. When analyzing the semantics of the words and phrases used in the sample of *Toronto Star* articles selected, the language used to describe people as 'blacks', 'whites', 'brown' or 'other' illustrates a discourse about 'race' coded within our normalized mythic assumptions about the world we live in. The language of 'race' used in these samples is a part of how the journalistic essence of visualization (Ericson et al., 1987) subtly socializes a mass audience to a dominant view on the reality of racial difference.

If you recall a central premise to this thesis, 'race' as a product of racism (Darder & Torres, 2004). *The Star's* coding of 'race' inverts this premise to read racism as a product of 'race'. As a result, 'race' as a natural fact is taken-for-granted as knowledge and appears obvious, to a given society, through their everyday use of language. Moreover, *The Star* insinuates that racism must be dealt with by exposing the practices of racial profiling that hinder meaningful social relations among the distinct 'races' that exist. As illustrated through samples of sentences taken from the five aforementioned articles, *The Star* uncritically reproduces common racial categories when reporting the practice of racial profiling by taking-for-granted that such categories are natural. This occurs through the abundant use of a normalized language about 'race'.

The language of 'race', used in the *Toronto Star's* series, illustrates how people can be read as texts by virtue of their physical features. The body, as a text, is encoded and decoded through a racialized language. It is interesting to note, however, that when it is overtly represented, 'race' falls into either the category of 'black' or 'white'. No other 'races' exist within these samples, with the exception of 'brown' or 'other' in samples 3 and 5. According to these examples, "brown is used to refer to people of South Asian descent while 'other' mainly represents people of Chinese and other Far Eastern origins". The terms 'brown' and 'other' do not necessarily represent a 'race' as much as they represent nationality or geographical origin. This is seen where the terms like 'brown' and 'other' must be qualified or anchored by a secondary definition to clear up any possibility for confusion. The fact that they are written in quotations connotes arbitrariness to their label. 'Black' and 'white' on the other hand are part of our commonsense discursive vocabulary. They need not be encased in quotation marks. Furthermore, secondary definitions of 'black' and 'white' are deemed by *The Star* to be unnecessary. As a result, 'black' and 'white' are not defined anywhere in the above passages nor are they defined anywhere in the entire series.

Notions of 'black' and 'white' are signifiers of social status that bear the weight of social, historical, and political significance. As cultural descriptors, skin colours are meshed within a larger framework of knowledge that constitutes dominant social myths. These myths carry second-order signification that validate a social relation of power.

A person is not just 'black' in complexion, but bears the burden of representing a larger community in everything they do. For example, when *The Star* refers to a racialized community, they refer to 'the black community' – as though it exists as an absolute homogeneous whole. Furthermore, when they refer to leaders of these racialized communities, they refer to them as 'black leaders' – as though there is only one type of racialized leader to represent one type of racialized community. On the contrary you do not see discourses that refer to 'white' communities or 'leaders of white communities'. The category of 'white' constitutes individuals within a population as opposed to 'black' constituting a segregated community within a population. This subtle distinction can lead to more overt generalizations of 'race' being attributed to crime.

When coupled with crime, 'black' can conjure images of deviant characters like Bigger Thomas – Richard Wright's *Native Son* (Wright, 1998). Such images bear the weight of an entire group of people as programmed deep within the dominant psyche of a racist society, multicultural or not. In this type of society, 'Black' signifies a type of person opposite and unequal to one who is 'white'. Although there are many contested narratives and meanings behind 'black' (Riggs, 1995), through myth, the sign 'black man' is reduced to a homogenized, second-order signifier for the behaviour and capabilities of most men who are perceived as 'black'. This is precisely what Frantz Fanon (1967) refers to as being trapped in his body. Although *The Star's* coverage of the issues appears to side with the victims of profiling, nowhere in its coverage is 'race' discredited as a natural or causal factor.

By perpetuating the myth that entire populations can be grouped by skin colour as a signifier of 'race', *The Star* inadvertently leaves behavioural assumptions linked to 'race' open for debate. The easiest way to avoid this debate would have been to address the notion of 'race' as a social construct that is produced through racism in the process of racialization. Nowhere in over 100 articles on the issue, is the notion of 'race' or the use of racial categories critically discussed as a factor of systemic racism. By not critically questioning the validity of racial categorizations as definitive group signifiers, *The Star* perpetuates the myth that 'race' is a fixed cultural category. As ideologically charged signifiers, myths about 'race' are constructed in and through language. Indeed, there is nothing fixed or natural about 'race' therefore it cannot be considered a cultural, much less, biological reality

X. MOVING BEYOND 'RACE'

CONCLUSION – Putting to rest the 'Strange Fruits' of our Past in the Present

> *Thus one of the greatest jokes in the world is the spectacle of whites busy escaping blackness and becoming darker everyday, and the blacks striving towards whiteness, becoming quite dull and grey.*
> (Ellison, 1947, p. 577)

Despite my findings and the fact that most progressive social scientists refrain from employing the construct of 'race' as a determinant of specific social phenomena (McLaren & Torres, 1999; San Juan Jr., 2002), discussions of 'race' – as a fixed analytical and descriptive category – continue to dominate popular and media discourses. Despite the fact that notions of 'race' have no basis in science, *The Star's* coverage of Philippe Rushton and racial profiling, abound with rigid conceptions of 'race'. Contrary to this coverage, *The Star's* reporting on the genetic discoveries that disprove such rigid classification of 'race' has been scarce. Such rigid characterizations are also prevalent in the 'official' narratives of Canadian multiculturalism that attempt to define and categorize citizens into clearly delineable groupings under the rubric of 'difference'. This notion of 'difference', couched in the broader 'liberal' discourse of tolerance and diversity, however, continues to reinscribe 'race' as a fixed cultural category. Moreover, such formulations tend to contain the vestiges of colonialist legacies (Bannerji, 2000).

In short, popular myths about 'race', as they have become institutionalized and canonized in 'official' notions of multiculturalism and perpetuated through consciousness producing industries like the mass media, continue to obscure existing power relations and power structures (San Juan, Jr., 2002; Meyerson, 2000). This engenders an environment that implicitly privileges certain communities at the expense of others through lived racialized beliefs and practices such as those seen through the policies of 'official multiculturalism' and practices of racial profiling. These beliefs and practices, however, are premised on a flawed notion of 'race'.

As discussed throughout this thesis, 'race' is a product of myth: an ideologically-loaded, discursive construct, manifest through language and produced in social relations of power. Seeing that 'races' come from racism (Darder & Torres, 2004), the myths that produce 'race' in social relations of power, constitute a conception of racism as a way of life. Indeed, racism as a way of life implies a process of socialization that normalizes our everyday thoughts and actions about fixing differences.

The process of socialization that institutionalizes categories of racial difference – sometimes referred to as racialization – is seldom analyzed in a critical fashion. Instead, racism is often talked about as an important social problem experienced through the isolated actions of individuals and organizations. When narrowly conceptualized this way, racisms are often examined through trivial fixations on reified notions of 'race'. As a result, racism as a problematic way of living has yet to be remedied. This is based on the homogenization and trivialization of the premise that we construct about it.

Moving forward, if racism is something that we truly want to rid society of; we need to attune our focus not on 'race' but on the processes of socialization (racialization) that impel its effects. As a collective society, we need to come together not as divergent individuals, preserved in a static sea of difference, but as conversation partners (Benhabib, 2002) united to solve a common crisis. We need to find ways in which to communicate more effectively towards a counter-socialization that can destroy 'racisms' at its root. Although there are currently no standardized formulae for dismantling 'racisms', solutions to social problems are dialectical and can only occur through participatory democratic intervention that recognize the hybridity of cultural identities.

This cannot currently be achieved through policies of 'official multiculturalism' nor can it be achieved through the constant barrage of media texts that reinforce imagined differences.

'Official multiculturalism', premised on the preservation of cultural wholes, presents more harm than good by managing difference as a social problem. As a result, the fixing of cultural differences and the reification of 'race' has led some scholars to revaluate and abandon the concept of multiculturalism in favour of polyculturalism. Instead of 'tolerating' or managing fixed racial or cultural differences, polyculturalism recognizes the plurality and fluidity of cultures. Cultures in this sense are seen as living, hybrid entities in the constitution of identity as a work in progress (Albert & Podur, 2003; Kelley, 2003). The media, however, continue to portray cultural differences contrary to a more fluid notion of culture.

Throughout the selected *Toronto Star* articles analyzed, 'race' has been coded as a fixed, cultural and biological entity. This is seen through its coverage of the Philippe Rushton as well as its exposé on racial profiling as practiced by the police force. Curiously enough, however, the one subject of news that was grossly underrepresented was *The Star's* scarce coverage of developments in genetic research that disprove common notions about 'race'. It is interesting to note that *The Star's* coverage on the genetic evidence occurred between its coverage on Rushton and its coverage on racial profiling. The fact that *The Star* continued to report on 'race' the same ways after its publication of the genome evidence as it had before its publication, is rather telling about the selective nature of its institutional memory.

Even years after its original series on 'Race and Crime', issues of racial profiling have resurfaced. This time reports come from the city of Kingston Ontario instead of

Toronto, where the Kinston Police Service has provided their own study that admits to the practice of racial profiling. A May 28th 2005 article published in the *Toronto Star* echoes the same reporting tactics as seen in its original series on 'Race and Crime' that occurred three years ago. As seen in this most recent article, *The Star* continues to code 'race' uncritically, as a rigid statement of fact. This indicates that little has progress has occurred in the ways in which we categorize each other. We still continue to live the myths of social difference through rigid categories of 'race'. As a result, further study should be dedicated towards theorizing alternative models to the ways in which we live the myths of social differences through notions of 'race'.

As a collective problem, in which all citizens have a stake, individual solutions are often inadequate and will not occur overnight. Seeing that this problem requires collective solutions, which push for a counter-socialization stemming from a critical consciousness, change will involve a process on the level of evolutionary proportions to re-naturalize a new world view. As daunting as this task may seem, the battle can only be won in small victories. These victories are evidenced in the various struggles and accomplishments for civil rights that have led to models of critical race theories, feminism, anti-corporate globalization movements and the like. The struggle towards social justice, however, did not begin and end with these models and theories. What are required now, in the changing face of newer 'racisms', are models and theories that can directly address the constantly evolving issues that the new 'racisms' create. Such models should stress the fact that 'racisms' cannot be dismantled through 'race' but should guide policies that addresses the roots of the problem through close attention to racialization.

To invoke the horticultural metaphor once more, 'races' are the 'strange fruits' that the trees of racisms produce. Like weeds, these trees continue to grow through 'biopower' (Foucault, 2003), choking off the life of other vegetation guided by acceptance, equality, and justice in the process. One cannot solve this problem by solely concentrating on plucking the fruit. One must essentially uproot the entire tree. In order to do so, one must learn to visualize the scope of the problem at the root and not by the fruits that the problem produces.

Visualization, structured in the process of socialization through myth, requires a counter-process of critical consciousness to affect these desired changes. As a dominant industry of visualization, the mass media are avenues where a counter-socialization movement must begin. Unfortunately at present, however, the media still view 'race' as distinguishable, via naturally distinct cultural and bio-genetic traits. The ways in which they continue to effect a visualization of this conception, contributes to the production of our dominant social perception that becomes normalized through myth. The mass media, therefore, as a site for the production, reproduction, and transformation of ideologically loaded myths, harbour our dominant perceptions of 'race'. This is particularly evident in *The Star's* practice of racial profiling in its reporting of Philippe Rushton and its coverage of racial profiling that the Toronto Police Service carries out.

Through *The Star's* accusations that racial profiling exists, the issues of racism become compounded. This occurs primarily because *The Star's* series on 'Race and Crime' misses the opportunity, in their coverage of racial profiling, to explore the roots of racism's social mechanisms by the ways in which it participates in a dominant discourse about 'race'. Although the *Toronto Star* was in the vanguard in its coverage of 'race' and crime, in the way that its investigation into racial profiling practiced by TPS exhibited a critical step towards exposing the pervasiveness of systemic racism, it merely scratched the surface of social issues deeply rooted in the historical context of power relations.

Functioning within the dominant myths about the reality of 'race' the *Toronto Star* ultimately succeeds in preserving the existing racial categories as commonsense delineations of a Canadian multicultural imaginary. These notions of 'race' – cultural and 'scientific' – legitimated and institutionalized through 'official multiculturalism' in Canada contribute to a form of apartheid that is ultimately restrictive to equality and justice for all citizens within Canada's borders. This further illustrates the ways in which vestiges of a colonialist legacy have found a home in the broader 'liberal' notion of tolerable difference.

Inscribed within the rhetoric of 'official multiculturalism' in Canada, the 'strange fruit' of this legacy survives in the *Toronto Star's* representation of 'race'. Rooted in racist colonial ideologies, the 'strange fruit' of these representations are manifest in the myths of our seemingly fixed and divided existence. As a result, the media have a large role in determining and reinforcing how groups are distinguished in difference to one another by the myths that they propagate. By focusing less on the fruit of 'race' and more on its roots through the process of racialization, the mass media have an important role to play in communicating and teaching anti-racist discourses towards social justice.

It is important to note, however, that racisms are not restricted to the overt phenomena of individual actions, nor are they restricted to the 'liberal' ideologies that inform a Canadian imaginary. Moving forward, a burgeoning field of literature is emerging in assessing the intimate relationships between modern forms of racism and contemporary trends towards globalization (Hardt & Negri, 2000; Marable, 2004; San Juan Jr., 2002). Studying these phenomena on a critical level will present unique and original challenges that I believe to have merit in deconstructing barriers in the journey towards a global social justice. Without tackling racism as a global issue, where everyone has a stake in its resolution, it becomes all the more difficult to uproot its existence from a more local Canadian perspective. I find it particularly fitting to end at this juncture with a quote from the late Dr. Martin Luther King Jr. (Dorrel, 2002)

Injustice anywhere, is a threat to justice everywhere.

References

A weak reaction to academic fraud. (1989, March 9). *The Toronto Star*, p. A28.

Achbar, M. & Wintonick, P. (1992). *Manufacturing Consent: Noam Chomsky and the Media*. Zeitgeist Video.

Adelman, L. et al. (2003). *Race – The Power of an Illusion*. California Newsreel.

Agger, B. (1992). *Cultural Studies as Critical Theory*. London: The Falmer Press.

Albert, M. & Podur, J. (2003). Revolutionizing Culture. *Znet*. Retreived January 10, 2005 from http://www.zmag.org/content/print_article.cfm?itemID=3914&sectionID=30

Allen, R. (2004). Whiteness and Critical Pedagogy. *Educational Philosophy and Theory*, 36(2), 121-136.

Allen, T. W. (1998). Summary of the Argument of "The Invention of the White Race". *Culture Logic*, (1) 2. Retrieved April 26, 2005 from http://eserver.org/clogic/1-2/allen.html

Allen, T. W. (1994). *The Invention of the White Race: The Origins of Oppression in Anglo America*. London: Verso.

American Institute of Physics (n.d.). Retrieved May 19, 2005 from http://www.aip.org/history/heisenberg/p01.htm

Anderson, B. (1991). *Imagined Communities: Reflections on the Origin and Spread of Nationalism*. London: Verso.

Appiah, K. A. (1995). Race. In F. Lentricchia & T. McLaughlin (Eds.) *Critical Terms for Literary Study* (274-287). Chicago: University of Chicago Press.

Balibar, E. (2002a). The Nation Form: History and Ideology. In P. Essed & D.T. Goldberg (Eds.) *Race Critical Theories* (220-230). Malden: Blackwell Publishers.

Balibar, E. (2002b). Reflections on "The Nation Form: History and Ideology". In P. Essed & D.T. Goldberg (Eds.) *Race Critical Theories* (413-416). Malden: Blackwell Publishers.

Bamshad, M.J. & Olsen, S.E. (2003). Does Race Exist? *Scientific American.Com*. Retrieved March 21, 2004 from http://www.sciam.com/article.cfm?articleID=00055DC8-3BAA-1FA8-BBAA83414B7F0000

Bannerji, H. (2000). *The Dark Side of the Nation: Essays on Multiculturalism, Nationalism and Gender*. Toronto: Canadian Scholars' Press.

Barbour, I. (1990). *Religion in an Age of Science: The Gifford Lectures, Volume One*. New York: HarperCollins.

Barker, M. (2002). The Problems with Racism. In P. Essed & D.T. Goldberg (Eds.) *Race Critical Theories* (80-89). Malden: Blackwell Publishers.

Barthes, R. (1996). Denotation and connotation. In P. Cobley (Ed.) *The Comminication Theory Reader* (129-133). London: Routledge.

Barthes, R. (1984). Myth Today. Taken from *Mythologies*. New York: Hill and Wang. Retreived January 26, 2004 from http://www.artsci.wustl.edu/~marton/myth.html

Barthes, R. (1972). *Mythologies*. New York: Hill and Wang.

Barthes, R. (1968). *Elements of Semiology*. New York: Hill and Wang. Retreived January 26, 2004 from http://www.marxists.org/reference/subject/philosophy/works/fr/barthes.htm

Bell, V. (2002). Reflections on "The End of Antiracism". (P. Gilroy) In P. Essed & D.T. Goldberg (Eds.) *Race Critical Theories* (509-512). Malden: Blackwell Publishers.

Benhabib, S. (2002). *The Claims of Culture: Equality and Diversity in the Global Era*. Princeton, New Jersey: Princeton University Press.

Bhabha, H. (2002). Of Mimicry and Man: The Ambivalence of Colonial Discourse. In P. Essed & D.T. Goldberg (Eds.) *Race Critical Theories* (113-122). Malden: Blackwell Publishers.

Bissoondath, N. (2002). *Selling Illusions: The Cult of Multiculturalism in Canada*. Toronto: Penguin Books.

Bohmer, P. (n.d.). Radical Theories of Racism and Racial Inequality: Marxist and Internal Colonialism. *Znet*. Retrieved January 10, 2005 from http://www.zmag.org/CrisesCurEvts/bohmerrace.htm

Bosmajian, H.A. (1974). *The Language of Oppression*. Washington: Public Affairs Press.

Bourne, J. (2002). Racism, Postmodernism and the Flight from Class. In D. Hill, P. McLaren, M. Cole & G. Rikowski (Eds.) *Marxism Against Postmodernism in Educational Theory* (195-210). Lanham, MD: Lexington Books.

Bove, P.A. (1995). Discourse. In F. Lentricchia & T. McLaughlin (Eds.) *Critical Terms for Literary Study* (50-65). Chicago: University of Chicago Press.

Boyd, R. (1996, October 13). Scientists find we are all same under the skin. No genetic basis for race, say researchers. *The Toronto Star,* p. A4.

Brace, C.L. (2000). Does Race Exist? An antagonist's perspective. *Nova Online.* Retrieve March 21, 2004 from
http://www.pbs.org/wgbh/nova/first/brace.html

Breton, R. (1999). Intergroup Competition in the Symbolic Construction of Canadian Society. In P.S. Li (Ed.) *Race and Ethnic Relations in Canada* (291-310). Toronto: Oxford University Press.

Buist, S. (2000). The Race–Research Funder. *Institutions: Institute for the Study of Academic Research.* Retrieved March 15, 2005 from
http://www.ferris.edu/isar/Institut/pioneer/rushton.htm

Cabusao, J.A. (2005). "Review of E. San Juan Jr.'s Racism and Cultural Studies" *Culture Logic.* Retrieved February 13, 2005 from
http://www.eserver.org/clogic/2005/cabusao.html

Callinicos, A. (1993). *Race and Class.* London: Bookmarks Publications.

Canadian Heritage. (n.d.). *Multiculturalism.* Retrieved April 10, 2005 from
http://www.pch.gc.ca/progs/multi/reports/ann2002-2003/01_e.cfm

Chomsky, N. (2002). In P.R. Mitchell & J. Schoeffel (Eds.) *Understanding Power: The Indispensible Chomsky.* New York: The New Press.

Clarke, A. (1992). Public Enemies: Police Violence and Black Youth. In *Point of View.* Toronto: Harper Collins Publishers Ltd.

Cohan, S. & Shires, L. (1996). Theorizing language. In P. Cobley (Ed.) *The Comminication Theory Reader* (115-125). London: Routledge.

Cox, O.C. (1959). *Caste, class, & race; a study in social dynamics.* New York: Monthly Review Press.

Daniels, R. (1996). Racism: Past and Present. *Znet.* Retrieved January 10, 2005 from
http://www.zmag.org/zmag/articles/oct96daniels.htm

Darder, A. & Torres, R. (2004). *After Race.* New York: New York University Press.

Day, R. (1998). Constructing the Official Canadian: A Geneology of the Mosaic Metaphor in State Policy Discourse. *Topia: Canadian journal of Cultural Studies.* (2), 42-66.

Deane, S. (1995). Imperialism/ Nationalism. In F. Lentricchia & T. McLaughlin (Eds.) *Critical Terms for Literary Study* (354-368). Chicago: University of Chicago Press.

Defleur, M. & Ball-Rokeach, S. (1989). *Theories of Mass Communication.* New York: Longman.

Dellinger, B. (1995). Critical Discourse Analysis of Media Texts. Retrieved January 15, 2004 from http://users.utu.fi/bredelli/cda.html

Dorrel, F. (2002). *What I've Learned About U.S. Foreign Policy: The War Against the Third World.* Retrieved April 10, 2005 from http://www.addictedtowar.com

D'Souza, D. (1995). *The End of Racism: Principles for a Multiracial Society.* New York: The Free Press.

Eagleton, T. (1991). *Ideology: An Introduction.* London: Verso.

Eco, U. (1996). How culture conditions the colours we see. In P. Cobley (Ed.) *The Comminication Theory Reader* (148-171). London: Routledge.

Ellison, R. (1990). *Invisible Man.* New York: Vintage International.

Ericson, R., Baranek, P., Chan, J. (1987). *Visualizing Deviance: A Study of News Organization.* Toronto: University of Toronto Press.

Essed, P. (2002). Everyday Racism: A New Approach to the Study of Racism. In P. Essed & D.T. Goldberg (Eds.) *Race Critical Theories* (176-194). Malden: Blackwell Publishers.

Eze, E.C. (2001). *Achieving our Humanity: The Idea of the Postracial Future.* New York: Routledge.

Fanon, F. (1967). *Black Skin White Masks.* New York: Grove Press.

Fiske, J. (1990). *Introduction to Communication Studies.* London: Routledge

Follow Kingston's lead. (2005, May 28). *The Toronto Star,* p. F6.

Foster, C. (1996). *A Place Called Heaven: The Meaning of Being Black in Canada.* Toronto: HarperCollins Publishers Ltd.

Foucault, M. (2003). *"Society Must be Defended": Lectures at the College de France 1975-76.* New York: Picador.

Frankenberg, R. (1993). *White Women, Race Matters: The Social Construction of Whiteness.* Minneapolis: University of Minnesota Press.

Freire, P. (1970). *Pedagogy of the Oppressed.* New York: The Seabury Press.

Friendly, M. (2002). Analysis of Toronto Police Database. Retrieved January 12, 2004 from http://thestar.com/static/PDF/021211_policeDB.pdf

Furumoto, K. B. (2002). Reflections on "Of Mimicry and Man: The Ambivalence of Colonial Discourse". (H. Bhabha) In P. Essed & D.T. Goldberg (Eds.) *Race Critical Theories* (426-432). Malden: Blackwell Publishers.

Gaines, E. (2001). Semiotic Analysis of Myth: A Proposal for an Applied Methodology. *American Journal of Semiotics.* 17(2). Retrieved January 10, 2004 from http://www.wright.edu/~elliot.gaines/analysisofmyth.htm

Gergen, K. (1991). *The Saturated Self.* USA: Basic Books

Gill, G.W. (2000). Does Race Exist? A proponent's perspective. *Nova Online.* Retrieved March 21, 2004 from http://www.pbs.org/wgbh/nova/first/gill.html

Gilroy, P. (2002). The End of Antiracism. In P. Essed & D.T. Goldberg (Eds.) *Race Critical Theories* (249-264). Malden: Blackwell Publishers

Gimenez, M. (2001). Marxism and class, gender and race: Rethinking the Trilogy. *Race, Gender & Class,* 8(2), 23-33

Giroux, H. (1995). White Panic. *Znet.* Retrieved January 12, 2005 from http://www.zmag.org/zmag/articles/mar95giroux.htm

Goldberg, D.T. (2002a). Modernity, Race, and Morality. In P. Essed & D.T. Goldberg (Eds.) *Race Critical Theories* (283-306). Malden: Blackwell Publishers.

Goldberg, D.T. (2002b). Reflections on "Modernity, Race, and Morality". In P. Essed & D.T. Goldberg (Eds.) *Race Critical Theories* (422-425). Malden: Blackwell Publishers.

Goldberg, D.T. & Essed, P. (2002). From Racial Demarcations to Multiple Identifications. In P. Essed & D.T. Goldberg (Eds.) *Race Critical Theories* (1-14). Malden: Blackwell Publishers.

Gramsci, A. (1992). *Prison Notebooks.* New York: Columbia University Press.

Greenblat, S. (1995). Culture. In F. Lentricchia & T. McLaughlin (Eds.) *Critical Terms for Literary Study* (225-232). Chicago: University of Chicago Press.

Hall, S. (2002a). Race, Articulation, and Societies Structured in Dominance. In P. Essed & D.T. Goldberg (Eds.) *Race Critical Theories* (38-68). Malden: Blackwell Publishers.

Hall, S. (2002b). Reflections on "Race, Articulation, and Societies Structured in Dominance". In P. Essed & D.T. Goldberg (Eds.) *Race Critical Theories* (449-454). Malden: Blackwell Publishers.

Hall, S. (1997). *Representation and the Media.* Media Education Foundation.

Hall, S. (1996). *Race, the Floating Signifier.* Media Education Foundation.

Hall, S. (1995). The Whites of Their Eyes; Racist Ideologies and the Media, In G. Dines & J. M. Humez (Eds.) *Gender, Race and Class in Media* (18-22). London: Sage Publications.

Hall, S. (1993). Encoding, decoding. In S. During (Ed.) *The Cultural Studies Reader* (90-103). New York: Routledge.

Hardt, M & Negri, A. (2000). *Empire.* Cambridge: Harvard University Press.

Henry, F. & Tator, C. (1999). State Policy and Practices as Racialized Discourse: Multiculturalism, the Charter, and Employment Equity. In P.S. Li (Ed.) *Race and Ethnic Relations in Canada* (88-115). Toronto: Oxford University Press.

Herman, E.S. (n.d.). Fog Watch: The New racist Onslaught. *Znet:* <http://www.zmag.org/zmag/articles/herman1.htm>

Herman, E.S. & Chomsky, N. (1988). *Manufacturing Consent: The Political Economy of the Mass Media.* New York: Pantheon Books.

Herrnstein, R.J. & Murray, C.A. (1994). *The Bell Curve: Intelligence and Class Structure in American Life.* New York: Free Press.

Hobsbawn, E. (1996). The Cult of Identity Politics. *New Left Review,* (217), 38-47.

Holt, T.C. (2000). *The Problem of Race in the Twenty-First Century.* Cambridge: Harvard University Press.

Hooks, B. (1995). "Challenging Capitalism & Patriarchy: Third World Viewpoint interviews Bell Hooks". *Znet.* Retrieved January 12, 2005 from http://www.zmag.org/zmag/articles/dec95hooks.htm

Hooks, B. (1997). *Cultural Criticism & Transformation.* Media Education Foundation.

Huckin, T. (n.d). Critical Discourse Analysis. In T. Miller (Ed.) *Functional Approaches to Written Texts: Classroom Applications.* US Department of State: English as a Foreign Language Publication Catalog. Retrieved January 26, 2005 from
http://exchanges.state.gov/education/engteaching/pubs/BR/functionalsec36.htm

Human Diversity Genome Project. (1999). Morrison Institute. Retrieved May 25, 2005 from http://www.stanford.edu/group/morrinst/hgdp/faq.html

Human Genome Project Information. (2000). Official White House press release. Retrieved May 25, 2005 from http://www.ornl.gov/sci/techresources/Human_Genome/project/clinton2.shtml

Hurst, L. (1989, January 28). An obstinate professor and his theories on race. Race superiority theories pure hokum, scientists say. *The Toronto Star,* pp. A1, A8.

Kavanagh, J. (1995). Ideology. In F. Lentricchia & T. McLaughlin (Eds.) *Critical Terms for Literary Study* (306-320). Chicago: University of Chicago Press.

Kelley, R. (2003). People in Me: "So What Are You?". *Znet.* Retrieved January 26, 2005 from http://www.zmag.org/content/print_article.cfm?itemID=3865&sectionID=30

Kellner, D. (1995a). *Media Culture: Cultural Studies, Identity and Politics.* London: Routledge.

Kellner, D. (1995b). Cultural Studies, Multiculturalism and Media Culture. In G. Dines & J. M. Humez (Eds.) *Gender, Race and Class in Media* (5-17). London: Sage Publications.

Kennedy, R. (2002). *"Nigger": The Strange Career of a Troublesome Word.* New York: Vintage Books.

Kuhn, T.S. (1962). *The Structure of Scientific Revolutions.* Chicago: University of Chicago Press.

Leonardo, Z. (2004). The Color of Supremacy: Beyond the discourse of "white privilege". *Educational Philosophy and Theory,* 36(2), 137-152.

Li, P. (1999a). Race and Ethnicity. In P.S. Li (Ed.) *Race and Ethnic Relations in Canada* (148-177). Toronto: Oxford University Press.

Li, P. (1999b). The Multiculturalism Debate. In P.S. Li (Ed.) *Race and Ethnic Relations in Canada* (3-20). Toronto: Oxford University Press.

Littlejohn, Stephen W. (1996). *Theories of Human Communication.* London: Wadsworth.

Lynn, M. (2004). Inserting the "Race" into Critical Pedagogy: An analysis of "race-based epistemologies". *Educational Philosophy and Theory,* 36(2), 153-166.

Makdisi, S. (2002). Reflections on "Imaginative Geography and Its Representations: Orientalizing the Oriental". (E. Said) In P. Essed & D.T. Goldberg (Eds.) *Race Critical Theories* (437-440). Malden: Blackwell Publishers.

Mallan, C. (2002, October 23). Racial bias 'a reality': Eves. Premier backs talks on treatment of blacks by police. *The Toronto Star*, p. A1.

Marable, M. (2004). Globalization and Racialization. *Znet*. Retrieved January 26, 2005 from http://www.zmag.org/content/print_article.cfm?itemID=6034&sectionID=30

Marcuse, H. (1969). *An Essay on Liberation*. Boston: Beacon Press.

Markus, M. (2002a). Cultural Pluralism and the Subversion of the "Taken-For-Granted" World. In P. Essed & D.T. Goldberg (Eds.) *Race Critical Theories* (392-412). Malden: Blackwell Publishers.

Markus, M. (2002b). Reflections on "Cultural Pluralism and the Subversion of the "Taken-For-Granted" World". In P. Essed & D.T. Goldberg (Eds.) *Race Critical Theories* (464-470). Malden: Blackwell Publishers.

Marx, K. (1970). *The German Ideology*. New York: International Publishers.

McCarthy, C. & Dimitriadis, G. (2004). Postcolonial Literature and the Curricular Imagination: Wilson Harris and the pedagogical implications of the carnivalesque. *Educational Philosophy and Theory*, 36(2), 201-214.

McGary, H. (2002). Reflections on "A Genealogy of Modern Racism". (C. West) In P. Essed & D.T. Goldberg (Eds.), *Race Critical Theories* (433-436). Malden: Blackwell Publishers.

McLaren, P. & Torres, R. (1999). Racism and multicultural education: Rethinking "race" and "whiteness" in late capitalism. IN S. May (Ed.) *Critical Multiculturalism: Rethinking Multicultural and Antiracist Education* (42-76). London: Falmer.

Melchers, R. (2003). Do Toronto Police Engage in Racial Profiling? *Canadian Journal of Criminology and Criminal Justice*, 45(3). Retrieved February 21, 2004 from http://www.utpjournals.com/product/cjccj/453/453_melchers.html

Menand, L. (1995). Diversity. In F. Lentricchia & T. McLaughlin (Eds.) *Critical Terms for Literary Study* (pp. 336-353). Chicago: University of Chicago Press.

Mensah, J. (2002). *Black Canadians: History, Experiences, Social Conditions*. Halifax: Fernwood Publishing.

Meyerson, G. (2000). "Rethinking Black Marxism: Reflections on Cedric Robinson and Others." *Cultural Logic*, 3(1/2). Retrieved March 15, 2005 from http://eserver.org/clogic/3-1%262/meyerson.html

Mitchell, B. (1989, March 15). Teachers condemn Rushton's theory of racial inferiority. *The Toronto Star*, p. A7.

Morrison, T. (2002). Black Matters. In P. Essed & D.T. Goldberg (Eds.) *Race Critical Theories* (265-282). Malden: Blackwell Publishers.

Omi, M. & Winant, H. (2002a). Racial Formation. In P. Essed & D.T. Goldberg (Eds.) *Race Critical Theories* (123-145). Malden: Blackwell Publishers.

Omi, M. & Winant, H. (2002b). Reflections on "Racial Formation". In P. Essed & D.T. Goldberg (Eds.) *Race Critical Theories* (455-459). Malden: Blackwell Publishers.

Ontario Human Rights Commission. (2003, October 21). *Paying the Price: The Human Cost of Racial Profiling*. Retrieved January 23, 2004 from http://www.ohrc.on.ca/english/consultations/racial-profiling-report.shtml

Ontario Ministry of Finance. (2001). *Census 2001 Highlights*. Retrieved February 15, 2005 from http://www.gov.on.ca/FIN/english/demographics/cenhi6e.htm

Parker, L. & Stovall, D. (2004). Actions Following Words: Critical race theory connects to critical pedagogy. *Educational Philosophy and Theory*, 36(2), 167-182.

Perry, M. (1992). *An Intellectual History of Modern Europe*. Boston: Houghton Mifflin.

Pieterse, J. N. (1995). "White Negroes". IN G. Dines & J. M. Humez (Eds.) *Gender, Race and Class in Media* (23-27). London: Sage Publications

Pieterse, J.N. (1992). *White on Black: Images of Blacks in Western Popular Culture*. New Haven, CT: Yale University Press.

Podur, J. (2002). *Znet Institutional Racism Instructional*. Retrieved January 15, 2005 from http://www.zmag.org/racewatch/znet_race_instructional.htm

Postel, D. (1997). An interview with Noel Ignatiev. *Znet*. Retrieved January 15, 2005 from http://www.zmag.org/zmag/articles/jan97postel.htm

Prince, A. (2001). *Being Black*. Toronto: Insomniac Press.

Quamina, O. (1996). *All Things Considered: Can We Live Together*. Toronto: Exile Editions.

Rankin, J., Quinn, J., Shephard, M., Duncanson, J., & Simmie, S. (2002, October 26). Black arrest rates highest. 'No one was born violent ... What's causing these problems?'. *The Toronto Star*, p. A15.

Rankin, J., Quinn, J., Shephard, M., Duncanson, J., & Simmie, S. (2002, October 20). Police target black drivers. Star analysis of traffic data suggests racial profiling. *The Toronto Star*, p. A8.

Rankin, J., Quinn, J., Shephard, M., Duncanson, J., & Simmie, S. (2002, October 19). Singled out. Star analysis of police crime data shows justice is different for blacks and whites. *The Toronto Star*, p. A1.

Razack, S. (2004a). *Dark Threats & White Knights: The Somalia Affair, Peacekeeping, and the New Imperialism.* Toronto: University of Toronto Press.

Razack, S. (2004b). When is Prisoner Abuse Racial Violence? *Znet.* Retrieved January 15, 2005 from http://www.duckdaotsu.org/racial_violence_abu_ghraib.html

Real, M. (1989). *Super Media: A Cultural Studies Approach.* London: Sage Publications.

Reed, A. (2000). *Class Notes.* New York: New Press.

Ricks, D. & Nelson, B. (2000, June 30). The other genome project. Search for human diversity proves we're all the same. *The Toronto Star*, p. F2.

Riggs, M. (1995). *Black Is ...Black Ain't.* California Newsreel

Roberts, J. & Gabor, T. (1989, March 14). Rushton's crime theories have no basis in fact. *The Toronto Star*, p. A21.

Rogers, P. (1992). *Aspects of Western Civilization: Problems and Sources in History, Volume 2.* New Jersey: Prentice-Hall, Inc.

Rushton, J. P. (2000). Is Race a Valid Taxonomic Construct? *The Occidental Quarterly*, 2(1). Retrieved January 14, 2004 from http://www.theoccidentalquarterly.com/vol2no1/jpr-taxonomic.html

Rushton, J. P. (1998). Race is More Than Just Skin Deep: A Psychologist's View. *Mankind Quarterly*, 39(2), 231-250. Retrieved January 14, 2004 from http://www.geocities.com/race_articles/rushton_view_race.html

Rushton, J.P. (1996). Statement on Race as a Biological Concept. *American Renaissance.* Retrieved January 14, 2004 from http://www.ameren.com/rushton.htm

Rushton, J. P. (1995a). Race and crime: an international dilemma. *Society,* 32(2)

Ruston, J.P. (1995b). *Race, Evolution and Behaviour: A Life History Perspective.* New Brunswick, New Jersey: Transaction Publishers.

Sahay, A. (1998). Transforming Race Matters: Towards a Critique-al Cultural Studies. *Cultural Logic,* 3(1/2). Retrieved March 21, 2005 from http://eserver.org/clogic/3-1%262/meyerson.html

Said, E. (2002). Imaginative Geography and Its Representations: Orientalizing the Oriental. In P. Essed & D.T. Goldberg (Eds.) *Race Critical Theories* (15-37). Malden: Blackwell Publishers.

Said, E. (1998a). *The Myth of 'The Clash of Civilizations'.* Media Education Foundation.

Said, E. (1998b). *On 'Orientalism'.* Media Education Foundation.

Said, E. (1993a). *Culture and Imperialism.* New York: Vintage Books.

Said, E. (1993b). Culture and Imperialism. Speech given at York University, Toronto, February 10, 1993. Retrieved January 15, 2004 from http://www.zmag.org/zmag/articles/barsaid.htm

Said, E. (1978). *Orientalism.* New York: Vintage Books

Sampson, H.F. (1967). *The Principle of Apartheid.* Johannesburg: Voortekkerpers.

San Juan Jr. E. (2003). "Marxism and the Race/Class Problematic: A Re-Articulation." *Culture Logic.* 6. Retrieved March 21, 2005 from http://eserver.org/clogic/2003/sanjuan.html

San Juan, Jr. E. (2002). *Racism and Cultural Studies: Critiques of Multiculturalist Ideology and the Politics of Difference.* Durham, North Carolina: Duke University Press.

Satzewich, V. (1999). The Political Economy of Race and Ethnicity. In P.S. Li (Ed.) *Race and Ethnic Relations in Canada* (311-346). Toronto: Oxford University Press.

Saussure, F. (1996a). The object of linguistics. In P. Cobley (Ed.) *The Comminication Theory Reader* (37-47). London: Routledge.

Saussure, F. (1996b). Linguistic value. In P. Cobley (Ed.) *The Comminication Theory Reader* (99-114). London: Routledge.

Scatamburlo-D'Annibale, V. & McLaren, P. (2004). Class Dismissed? Historical materialism and the politics of "difference". *Educational Philosophy and Theory*, 36(2), 183-200.

Scatamburlo-D'Annibale, V. & McLaren, P. (2003). The Strategic Centrality of Class in the Politics of "Race" and "Difference". *Cultural Studies, Critical Methodologies*, 3(2), 148-175.

Small, P. (2002, October 26). Black leaders want a say. Not consulted on Dubin move, they charge. *The Toronto Star*, p. B1.

Smith, D. (1989, February 17). Rushton called a racist at Geraldo taping. *The Toronto Star*, pp. A1, A2.

Shohat, E. & Stam, R. (1995). *Unthinking Eurocentrism; Multiculturalism and the Media*. London: Routledge.

Sollors, W. (1995). Ethnicity. In F. Lentricchia & T. McLaughlin (Eds.) *Critical Terms for Literary Study* (288-305). Chicago: University of Chicago Press.

Sontag, S. (2003). *Regarding the Pain of Others*. New York: Picador.

Spencer, S. (2002). Reflections on "Black Matters". (T. Morrison) In P. Essed & D.T. Goldberg (Eds.) *Race Critical Theories* (441-444). Malden: Blackwell Publishers.

Spivak, G. & Gunew, S. (1993). Questions of multiculturalism. In S. During (Ed.) *The Cultural Studies Reader* (193-202). New York: Routledge.

Street, P. (2002). A Whole Lott Missing: Rituals of Purification And Racism Denial. *Znet*. Retrieved January 12, 2005 from http://www.zmag.org/content/print_article.cfm?itemID=2784&sectionID=30

Turner, G. (1992). *British Cultural Studies: An Introduction*. New York: Routledge.

Tyler, T. (2003, June 25). Judge dismisses suit against the Star. Officers' union sought $2.7 billion Stories dealt with racial profiling. *The Toronto Star*, p. A1.

Ujimoto, K.V. (1999). Studies of Ethnic Identity, Ethnic Relations, and Citizenship. In P.S. Li (Ed.) *Race and Ethnic Relations in Canada* (253-290). Toronto: Oxford University Press.

Van Dijk, T. (2002a). Discourse, Knowledge, and Ideology. Retrieved January 10, 2004 from http://www.discourse-in-society.org/teun.html

Van Dijk, T. (2002b). Reflections on "Denying Racism: Elite Discourse and Racism". In P. Essed & D.T. Goldberg (Eds.) *Race Critical Theories* (481-485). Malden: Blackwell Publishers.

Van Dijk, T. (2000). New(s) Racism: A Discourse Analytical Approach. In *Ethnic Minorities and the Media* (33–49). UK: Open University Press.

Van Dijk, T. (1998). Critical Discourse Analysis. Retrieved January 10, 2004 from http://www.hum.uva.nl/~teun/cda.htm

Van Dijk, T. (1993). Denying Racism: Elite Discourse and Racism. In *Racism and Mitigation in Western Europe* (179-93). Oxford: Berg.

Wacquant, L. (2002). From Slavery to Mass Incarceration: Rethinking the "race question" in the US. *New Left Review,* 13, 41-60.

Walcott, R. (2003). *Black Like Who? Writing. Black. Canada.* Revised Second Ed. Toronto: Insomniac Press.

Wallace, M. (1993). Negative Images: towards a black feminist cultural criticism. In S. During (Ed.) *The Cultural Studies Reader* (118-134). New York: Routledge.

Weinfeld, M. & Wilkinson, L. (1999). Immigration, Diversity, and Minority Communities. In P.S. Li (Ed.) *Race and Ethnic Relations in Canada* (55-87). Toronto: Oxford University Press.

West, C. (2002). A Genealogy of Modern Racism. In P. Essed & D.T. Goldberg (Eds.) *Race Critical Theories* (90-112). Malden: Blackwell Publishers.

West, C. (1993). The new cultural politics of difference. In S. During (Ed.) *The Cultural Studies Reader* (203-220). New York: Routledge.

Wilden, T. (1980). *The Imaginary Canadian: An Examination for Discovery.* Vancouver: Pulp Press.

Winter, J. (2002). *Media Think.* Montreal: Black Rose Books.

Wise, T. (n.d.). Armed With a Loaded Footnote: Sloppy Statistics, Bogus Science and the Assault on Racial Equity. *Znet.* Retrieved January 15, 2005 from http://www.zmag.org/racewatch/loadfoot.htm

Wise, T. (n.d.). Blinded by the White: Crime, Race and Denial in America. *Znet.* Retrieved January 15, 2005 from http://www.zmag.org/zmag/articles/wise.htm

Wise, T. (n.d.). Color-Conscious, White-Blind: Race, Crime and Pathology in America. *Znet.* Retrieved January 15, 2005 from http://www.zmag.org/racewatch/colcons.htm

Wise, T. (1999). Exploring the Depths of Racist Socialization. *Znet.* Retrieved January 15, 2005 from http://www.zmag.org/zmag/articles/july99wise.htm

Wise, T. (1999). Of Hate Crimes, Big and Small. *Znet.* Retrieved January 15, 2005 from http://www.zmag.org/sustainers/content/1999-08/12wise.htm

Wright, R. (1998). *Native Son.* New York: Perennial Classics.

Appendix

Census Highlights

Ontario Ministry of Finance. (2003) *Census 2001 Highlights*. Retrieved February 15, 2005 from http://www.gov.on.ca/FIN/english/demographics/cenhi6e.htm

Visible Minorities Making Canada Increasingly Diverse

- Visible minorities are defined as persons, other than Aboriginal peoples, who are non-Caucasian in race or non-white in colour.

- Almost 4 million Canadians identified themselves as a visible minority in the 2001 Census, accounting for 13.4% of the total population. This was an increase from 1996 when the proportion was 11.2% and a major change from 1991 (9.4%) and 1981 (4.7%).

- At the provincial level, British Columbia had the highest proportion of visible minorities, representing 21.6% of its population, followed by Ontario at 19.1%.

- People of Chinese origin are Canada's largest visible minority group, with a population of more than one million. In 2001, they made up 3.5% of the country's population, followed by South Asians (3%) and Blacks (2.2%).

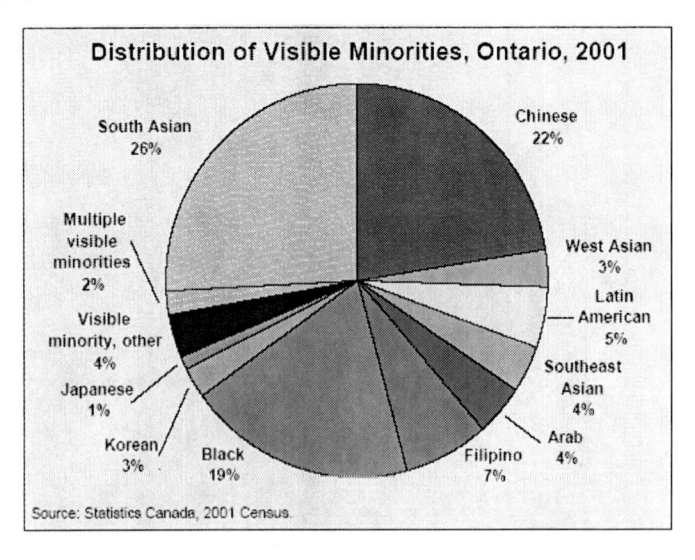

Distribution of Visible Minorities, Ontario, 2001

- South Asian 26%
- Chinese 22%
- Multiple visible minorities 2%
- West Asian 3%
- Visible minority, other 4%
- Latin American 5%
- Japanese 1%
- Southeast Asian 4%
- Korean 3%
- Arab 4%
- Black 19%
- Filipino 7%

Source: Statistics Canada, 2001 Census.

Ontario Home to 54% of Visible Minorities in Canada

- There were 2.2 million visible minority individuals in Ontario in 2001, accounting for 19.1% of the province's population. They represented 54% of all visible minorities in Canada.

- Among visible minority groups, South Asians (554,870) accounted for 26% of visible minorities, followed by Chinese (481,505) at 22%, and Blacks (411,095) at 19%.

- In 1991, Blacks were the largest visible minority group (311,000 or 3.1% of total population), with Chinese second (290,400 or 2.9%), followed by South Asians (285,600 or 2.9%).

February 5, 2003

Office of Economic Policy
Labour and Demographic Analysis Branch [21]

---

21 Please note that the webpage referenced in this appendix has been edited to fit the format of this page, keeping only the information pertinent to this thesis. For the full webpage, please refer to the website referenced at the top of this appendix.

Vita Auctoris

Rawle Gavin Agard was born June 24th 1975 in Georgetown Guyana. He immigrated to Canada with his parents in 1977 where they lived in Toronto, North York, and Scarborough before eventually settling in Pickering Ontario. He graduated from Dunbarton High school in Pickering and eventually went on to complete his Bachelor of Arts in Communication Studies at the University of Windsor in 1998. Although he is currently a candidate for the Master of Arts degree at the University of Windsor – with hopes of graduating in the spring of 2005 – he is looking forward to starting a Doctor of Philosophy degree in Media Studies at the University of Western Ontario in the fall of 2005.